How to Source a Contract Manufacturer

By William F. X. Madden, III

TRAIN OF THOUGHT
P R E S S

Publisher's Note

This book is designed to provide information and motivation to our readers. It is sold with the understanding that the publisher is not engaged to render any type of legal, financial, tax, or any other kind of professional advice. No warranties or guarantees are expressed or implied by the publisher's choice to include any of the content in this volume. No fiduciary relationship is established. Neither the publisher nor the individual author shall be liable for any physical, psychological, emotional, financial, or commercial damages, including, but not limited to, special, incidental, consequential, or other damages. Our views and rights are the same: You are responsible for your own choices, actions, and results.

ISBN: 978-0-9907728-9-7

Summary: Advice on how to source a contract manufacturer.

Connie Johnston
Train of Thought Press
2275 Huntington Drive, #306
San Marino, CA 91108
www.TrainOfThoughtPress.com

TRAIN OF THOUGHT
P R E S S

Dedication

I would like to dedicate this book to the following people:

My father, the best man I have ever known.

The woman who cost me six figures and the one who drives me to make seven.

To my two beautiful children, you are the love of my life.

Acknowledgements

I would like to thank all my clients who have made this possible. If it wasn't for Doug, Roy, JJ, Brian, Helen, Ethan, Jordan, Lauren and Tapan I never would have actually finished this book.

I would like to thank all of the horrible contract manufacturers, without you this book wouldn't be necessary.

Finally, Dave, Jim, Jeff, Sean and Byron thank you so much for all your help in life. If you ever need anything I am always a call away.

My mother and Mary, thank you for all the support over the years.

Table of Contents

Introduction

If you are reading this book, you are one of three types of people:

1. A person who has always thought that their "product X" (your grandmother's sauce, your chocolate recipe, etc.) was great, but doesn't even know where to start to find a contract manufacturer.

2. A person who has been looking for the "needle in the haystack" (contract manufacturer) for the last 6 months.

3. A person who has been manufacturing the product themselves and realizes that this is a huge distraction and financial suck.

This book is for all three types of people.

My name is Will Madden, and I've worked in the food industry for the past 18 years. I know the industry inside and out and have seen it all. I've helped startups and multimillion-dollar businesses find the perfect contract manufacturers, setting them up for long-term success.

However, I recognize that not everyone is able to afford my consulting fees. Or perhaps you're a true Do-It-Yourselfer and figure you will give it a try. Whatever your situation, this guide is designed to educate you on the process of sourcing a contract manufacturer for the food industry.

This book is written in plain, easy-to-understand English. I am not a professional writer, but you'll see that I know my stuff, and I can save you a truckload of trouble if you'll listen to what I have to say.

In fact, I'd like to begin this book with a disclaimer. You know, like the disclaimers you see on diet pill labels, saying "Not FDA Approved". Here it is:

At times while reading this book, you may find yourself thinking something along the lines of, "Man... this Will Madden sure is an arrogant prick."

I want you to be aware that I know this. Some of the things I'm going to say in here may rub you the wrong way, and for that, I apologize. My hope is that by the end of this book, you will start thinking things like, "Man... this Will Madden is a *likable* arrogant prick who actually knows this business inside and out. In fact, I want to buy this guy a couple of beers."

The other reason I've written this book in this style and tone is because frankly, this subject isn't the most exciting topic on the planet. At dinner parties, when people ask me what I do, their eyes glaze over if I don't spice it up a little. In fact, at times I just say I sell life insurance so I don't have to go into it. I'm warning you in advance: If you get offended by a minor swear word or two, you won't want to read this book. I curse for emphasis because sometimes there is no better way to say something—and it adds entertainment value. I'm hoping to get a chuckle out of you now and then.

Also, I will be honest, at times brutally so. I don't sugar coat things; I tell you how it really is. Because that's what you want to know, isn't it?

There are all kinds of bullshitters out there who will tell you, "You can make your dream come true!" without giving you a shred of useful information. They'll feed your optimism, but they'll just waste your time, money, and energy. I'm all about telling you what the truth is in this industry so you can determine if you have the drive, resources, and stones to get your dream business off the ground.

It is my hope that this book will truly help you. I know this industry well because I've worked on both sides of it, and I've negotiated enough contracts to have seen it all. I'll help you identify and avoid the pitfalls of the industry as you pursue your plans to establish or expand your business in the food industry.

Ready to do this thing?

Then let's get going.

Part I:
Understanding the Food Industry Landscape

If you've been thinking about starting your food business and are finally ready to take on this challenge, you are in luck. Your timing is impeccable. Want to know why?

Because right now small niche food businesses are the up-and-coming trend. Consequently, there is a ton of money going into the industry. They're the latest fad, the coolest thing.

Why?

Because all of the following trends are converging in your favor:

1. People all over the country are interested in supporting small businesses.

2. Local, organic, or small-batch products are considered premium.

3. Healthy alternatives to popular junk foods are big sellers.

Here's a real life example, something you can Google and read about right now to see that I'm not just blowing smoke up your ass. At this time (Winter 2015), Whole Foods is sponsoring an effort to support small, local, start-up food businesses. They've held workshops along with the city of Chicago with the Greater Engelwood Community Development Corporation through which they inspire small food companies to use commercial kitchens and apply for loans so they can launch their products and sell them in Whole Foods.

This isn't happening just in Chicago. Commercial kitchens and indie food companies are springing up all over the country. Grocery stores like Whole Foods, Earth Fare, and Publix are looking to buy from small niche food companies so they can cash in on this opportunity. Like any smart business, they are tracking consumer trends and trying to position themselves on the front end of the movement.

So you've got three things in your favor: timing, a positive business trend and a move toward health foods as opposed to junk foods. However, you'll need to consider a lot more than these three factors as you set out to start a business. Read on to learn what you need to know.

Chapter 1: Finding Your Way

As you get started, you'll quickly discover that you don't know what you don't know. It's my goal to help you figure out the basic lay of the land so you can navigate this tricky territory. That means you need to learn the terms people in the industry use and how to talk like someone who has been around the block a time or two. You need to know this information BEFORE you start approaching co-manufacturers.

Jargon
Before you speak to anyone in this industry, you need to familiarize yourself with the terminology. The following are terms you will use frequently when discussing your product.

3PL
Third party logistics- A **third-party logistics** provider (abbreviated **3PL**, or sometimes **TPL**) is a firm that provides service to its customers of outsourced (or **"third party"**) **logistics** services for part, or all of their supply chain management functions.

Commercialization
The process in which a product is taken from ideation to production.

R&D
Research and development. The process in which a concept is developed utilizing consumer insights and then vetted in the manufacturing process.

Timeline
The amount of time each step in the development process will take – includes ideation, refinement, sampling, trials and first production.

The Most Important Jargon in This Industry

It's important to understand that in this industry, people use the following terms interchangeably:

- Contract manufacturer
- Co-man

And...

- Contract packager
- Co-packer

You will want to familiarize yourself with these terms.

What's the difference between a co-man and a co-packer?

A co-man, or contract manufacturer, is somebody who actually manufactures a product for you. For example, Little Lady Foods is a pizza contract manufacturer. They make the dough, bake it, and put the toppings on. They're a manufacturer; they make your product for you.

A co-packer, or contract packager, is somebody who takes bulk product that has already been produced and packages it in a specified way. For example, perhaps you need club packs of cereal, multi-serves, or displays.

Take, for example, when you go to Costco and see three different types of cereal in one box. A contract packager takes in three different bulk types of cereal, packages each type of cereal in a specific size and type of packaging, and then puts one bag of each into a carton and seals the carton.

In summary: a co-man manufactures product, and a co-packer packages product in a specified way.

Generally, most small food companies won't work with both co-mans and co-packers. You may wind up working with both,

7

but most likely you'll work with a contract manufacturer (who will also package your product).

However, there are exceptions to this model. For example, if you're producing a specialized product like a certain type of salt or a tea that requires blending and packing, you'll use contract packagers because there's not really anything for the co-man to make. The co-packers blend a few things together and then they put it in a package.

Co-packers are also used in situations where the co-manufacturer's monster lines are moving product too fast to accommodate requirements like odd pack sizes (club packs and single serves, variety packs, etc.).

The following is an example from my own life. I used to work with a cereal company, but their manufacturing line was very fast and was designed only for a specifically-sized box of cereal. So whenever they had to produce single-serve packages for giveaways and promotions, they would send us full boxes of cereal that we would have to open, dump into a tote, and then repackage into those little single serves.

Understanding What Co-Manufacturers Do and Don't Do
You might still be confused about the roles of co-mans versus co-packers, but it's really not that complicated.

You will probably end up negotiating a contract with a contract manufacturer, and the arrangement will work loosely as follows.

Let's say you want to make beef jerky and sell it. You're going to tell the co-man, "I need beef jerky." So they're going to make the beef jerky, and then they are going to dry it or dehydrate it, whatever the process is.
Then they're going to take the finished product and put it in a package for you. They're going to hand it to you as a finished product, ready to sell.

The same process would happen if you were selling cookies. The co-man would make the dough, bake the cookies, and put them into a package so they were ready for sale.

Contract manufacturers actually make stuff, so the world is a lot wider for contract manufacturing than it is for contract packaging. Contract packaging isn't a value-added service; it's very commoditized, whereas contract manufacturing is a value-added service that is not highly commoditized.

If you want to learn more about this, you can read about it on the Contract Packaging Association's website or the Private Label Manufacturers' Association.

Situations in Which You Might Use a Co-Man *and* a Co-Packer
As I said, in most cases, you will end up working with a contract manufacturer. However, you might find a fantastic contract manufacturer who has great pricing and a wonderful delivery schedule. They may all be generally awesome people, but they aren't good at secondary packaging. This may result in an instance when you will need both a co-man and a co-packer.

1. You Have Unique Packaging Requirements

For example, let's say you want your product delivered in a certain style of packaging, and the co-man doesn't have the equipment to package product in that manner. The equipment might cost a million dollars. It doesn't make sense for the co-man to invest in that equipment just for your one product, or perhaps they don't have room for the equipment. So you go ahead and have your product carted to another guy who packages it.

Take granola bars, for instance. If you're at Quaker, you have 50 different types of variety packs. Your bars are flying off the line at a million bars per shift. You do not have the opportunity to slow down that line and bring product off the floor and put it in boxes to make a variety pack. Your line is so fast and so automated that it's just unfeasible to package it in-house.

So the co-man makes the granola bars, puts them into bulk boxes, and then sends them to another company who takes them and puts them into variety packs. They take one of this bar and one of that bar, and one of the third bar, and they make a variety pack.

Now, a contract manufacturer might do that for you if you're a small company and they are an equally small co-man. But if you're General Mills, it doesn't pay for you to do it yourself because you have to get that product up and out to market at record speed. So you'll send it to a contract packager who'll do the variety packs for you.

2. You Run Into a Product Discontinuation

Another situation that happens more often than you might imagine is product discontinuation by a buyer. Let's say you made variety packs of cereal specifically for Costco, but Costco discontinued the item. (Product discontinuation can happen for a variety of reasons, many of which have nothing to do with your product quality or pricing, and may very well be out of your control.)

Now you're sitting there with ten truckloads of cereal that's all packaged in club packs. You have two choices:

1. Severely discount the cereal (which may piss off Costco and ruin your chances with them for future deals) and get rid of the product through a fire sale, or

2. Bring the product back and have someone literally open up the boxes and repackage them, put them into cases, and sell them through normal channels.

A co-packer can pull off that repackaging job in no time. If you try repackaging on your own you will probably have a disaster on your hands.

As you can see, the roles of a co-man and co-packer can bleed into one another. As you get familiar with the way this industry works and get to know the major players, you'll begin to recognize when you need the services of one company instead of the other.

Summary: The Typical Set Up is You and a Co-Man

It's important to understand what both co-mans and co-packers do, but you'll probably only have to know this for the purposes of identifying which companies you'll want to approach (or avoid).

In most cases, you will start with a co-man, who will make and package your product for you. You probably won't need a co-packer unless your product takes off. Then you may need the co-packer for specialty packaging situations like the ones I mentioned above.

But I'm getting ahead of myself. Let me explain a few things about the food industry and sourcing a co-manufacturer that you'll need to know before you start making phone calls.

Chapter 2: Before You Even Start Looking for a Co-Man

There are a few things you need to know before you even consider looking for a co-man on your own. The following are the three most important.

1. It Takes Time
Finding a contract manufacturer takes time. If you know the industry well and you have connections, it can take anywhere from a few hours to a few weeks of work. This all depends on the scope and unique requirements of your product.

However, if you don't have connections in the industry, you should expect to get a loud "Thanks, but NO THANKS" from just about every co-man you approach. You can expect that you will have to knock on a lot of doors before one opens.

One mistake a lot of people make is thinking this is an easy task. Don't think that it will only take a day or two. Don't think that a simple Internet search and a few phone calls is going to land you a contract manufacturer, much less the best possible manufacturing deal.

I'll explain how to come across as an attractive client in a later chapter, which will cut down on the amount of time it will take for you to source a manufacturer. For now, you just need to tuck away this little gem: Finding a co-man is *hard*, and *it takes a long time*.

2. You Will Need Relationships Inside the Industry
I've been dealing with people in this industry for almost 20 years. I know everybody from junior buyers all the way up to presidents of billion-dollar organizations. I've worked with people who manufacture cereal, pizza, entrees… you name it, I've worked with them. I know a lot of people, and as a result, I have an extensive network in place.

If you're determined to do this on your own, you will need to network and build relationships. If you have friends in the food industry, start talking to them now. See if they know people, and find out if they have people who owe them a favor.

More importantly, see if they're willing to guide you through this mess. You'll have to network in this industry to find a good co-man who's willing to take you.

How I Built My Network

When I started helping people source, I was working for a small pizza contract manufacturer. I realized that buyers would come to you first if you could add additional value to the relationship. If I could tell people where to have something made (if the company I was working with couldn't do it), they would come to me with future opportunities. They recognized that I was in the know and able to find resources they couldn't. That's how I added value to the relationship, and that's when my extensive network began to form.

At the time, I was dealing with a major food company that contracted us to produce pizzas and with another major food company who also contracted with us to make pizzas but were also looking at getting into entrees. I networked with the first major company, found out who was manufacturing their entrées and who other possible sources were for excellent entrée production, and then I passed on that information to the second company. Later, when I had another company who wanted to make dough balls, I went to the second company and asked, "Who makes your dough balls?" They responded, telling me, "Oh, we go to so-and-so."

Over the years, I widened that network and became a very dependable resource. People would actually say in those organizations, "Oh, we're thinking about coming up with this. Have you talked to Will's company?" They'd come to me and I'd say, "Well, I can't do entrées very efficiently, but you can call this company."

As I developed that network, I enabled us to be the first-stop for a lot of companies, At first, I had to search like hell and ask other companies to find out who had the right capabilities, but, over time, my network grew. When I left that pizza company for a snack company, I continued to employ these same tactics. I was so successful there that I became the Director of New Business in less than two years, at the age of 31.

Now I've been at this for 18 years. I know what types of partnerships work and what types fail. I know the loopholes and weasel clauses to close. I can spot a bad contract from a mile away, and I know a lot of the tricks companies use to screw over the naïve newbies in the industry.

Just recently I had one of my clients call and tell me, "Yeah, you know this Project Y that we're working on?"

I assured him that I did.

He said, "I was talking with a guy who's the president of a division with another food company about who they use for that product. You know, asking him if he knew anyone who could produce that type of product."

The president of that food division told him, "Well, you can try these guys, but we always use Will Madden to help us find people."

The two of them laughed their asses off when he said, "So do we."

That's 18 years in the making. But the way it started was that I wanted to sell product, so I offered the following deal: If I couldn't make it for you, I'd find somebody who could. Through that, I developed the network that became Right Brain Consulting.

3. You Need to Know Your Product

If you've just been making your product in your kitchen, you need to forget looking for a co-man for now. You're not at the right stage in the game yet, and you've got some work to do before you start calling co-mans.

Why? You can't call up a co-man and say, "This is how I make it in my kitchen at home," because nobody else will ever make it that way. You need to find out what it takes to make your product on a commercial scale.

To learn what that means, in practical terms, read on. What you think is "commercial scale" is probably a drop in the bucket. I'll help you determine if you really need a co-man yet, and if so, what you need to do to prove you have enough experience to be taken seriously.

Because you want to be taken seriously, right? I thought so. Let's dive into the brass tacks of what that will require.

Summary: What You Need to Know

It takes time to research co-mans and to develop relationships in the industry. You also need to know your product and figure out how to scale production commercially. Make sure you figure out these three pieces of the puzzle before you consider approaching co-manufacturers.

Part II: The "I Have a Dream" People

In the beginning of this book, I described three types of people who approach me. We (those of us in the food industry) call two of these three types of people "I Have a Dream" people. They are:

1. A person who has always thought that his or her "product X" (your grandmother's sauce, your chocolate recipe, etc.) was great but doesn't even know where to start to find a contract manufacturer.

2. A person who has been looking for the "needle in the haystack" (contract manufacturer) for the last 6 months, but has been repeatedly turned down.

"I Have a Dream" people all face the same obstacle when looking for a co-manufacturer: **No one will take you seriously!**

This is the biggest problem you will face. Why? Because every contract manufacturer is approached by unfunded startups, every single day. So you are nothing special. Remember, this is the best idea *you* have ever heard of, but this is not *their* idea. It will not be their product.

All they want to do is make product and make money. You are the one with the dream, not them. You love the idea, and you probably believe it will be a smash hit or feel that it will change the world, but they won't feel the love unless you can prove that you are worth the investment.

Remember, at the end of this, if you are successful, you will be the one selling your great idea for multimillions... not them.

But in order to get to the point where you are selling your product, you have to get a co-man to work with you. And in order to get a co-man to work with you, you have to get them to notice you.

The following are the obstacles you must overcome in order to gain a co-man's confidence and get a little respect:

1. **You don't have a scalable, proven recipe.**
2. **You haven't got the financing worked out.**
3. **Nobody thinks your product is unique and special (except you).**
4. **You haven't even thought about branding your product.**
5. **You have no idea where you'll store or how you'll transport your product.**
6. **You have no clue how it should be packaged.**
7. **You don't know what regulations apply.**
8. **You don't have a business plan or proof that you are ready to scale.**

I know that probably sounds like a lot of negativity. Some of you may get pissed at me and just slam this book shut. (Or hit close on the e-book screen, which is admittedly less satisfying.)

Don't do that. I'm actually treating you with respect; I'm telling you how it really is so that you'll have a fighting chance.

If you are a parent, you will get this analogy:

If your kids are anything like mine, they have probably come to you at some point with some ridiculous scheme. Maybe your daughter wants to breed Burmese pythons in her bedroom and sell them on the Internet, and she thinks this will make her both famous and rich.

You, being the sane adult that you are, realize that it takes several grown men to handle a female Burmese python, never mind her mate and spawn. You also know that it is quite likely that a Burmese python would get out and eat the family cat, thus destroying your child's affinity for snakes and leaving you with the unpleasant task of re-homing aforementioned snake and mate. (And maybe even snake babies, which you would probably find out are not as easy to sell as your daughter has been led to believe.)

However, when you try to explain to your darling daughter that her plan has more holes in it than a fishing net, she will stomp her feet and insist that she has done her research on the Internet and knows everything there is to know about breeding and selling pythons. And she'll really mean it, too.

No matter how much you try to rationalize with her, your daughter will think you're just a meanie who doesn't like snakes. You know that you're being reasonable, but she doesn't see that you have her best interests in mind.

Likewise, I'm not trying to be a jerk. I'm *trying* to be nice to you. I want to save you the pain of investing everything you've got into this business, only to waste years of your time and thousands of dollars because you weren't properly prepared. I'm going to help you understand what obstacles are in the way so you go into this endeavor with your eyes wide open.

I'll also help you to understand what it takes to overcome these obstacles. In a sense, I'm stopping you from buying that breeding pair of Burmese pythons if you aren't ready to take on the responsibility. Just like Florida is overrun with exotic pets that have been set loose after their owners found out how huge a 16-foot snake really is, the world of startups is overflowing with failed food industry companies. I'm helping you learn everything you need to know so you can build a viable business, not become another sad statistic.

Each of the chapters in this section addresses the obstacles I mentioned above. Read on and learn, my friend. This is important stuff, and I truly want to help you avoid the mistakes that might make you give up on your dream.

Chapter 3: Why You Need a Scalable, Proven Recipe

Let's start with a story.

At one point, a business development specialist I often work with sent me a woman who wanted to make chips out of seaweed. She needed help finding a co-man, and I agreed to try to help her.

She had a formula that she had used at home to make them, and she thought she knew how to scale the recipe for commercial production. When I went out searching for co-manufacturers, I did a broad search of about 45 to 50 co-manufacturers that I knew well, and I got six or seven of them to actually try making the chips on test trials. Honestly, they did it because I knew these six or seven guys pretty well, and they had contracted for successful projects with me before, so they were willing to mess with somebody who had never done anything.

You can guess what happened, can't you? Batch after batch, the chips came out terrible. They were soggy.

Why did this happen? While she flash-fried for a couple of seconds, their lines were all set for 6, 12, 18, 30, 60, whatever-second fries, which made the product soggy when it came out.

I finally did find a guy who was able to look at the product and know what needed to be done. We lucked out by finding a co-man who would devote a little bit of time to the problem, and he figured out how to do it right. Now keep in mind, this kind of co-man is a rarity. He has a PhD in food science from a respectable university and loves a challenge.

Now, he spent a ridiculous amount of time trying to figure out how to make her product on commercial equipment, but then when he said, "To make this on a commercial scale, it'll cost you $9,000 in capital," she disappeared. *Poof* Into thin air. Quite the magic trick.

Of course, this totally pissed off that co-man. After all, he had invested a lot of time into figuring out how to produce her product. All for nothing.

(By the way, if $9,000 sounds like a lot of money, you're not ready to contract with a co-man yet. More on financing in the next chapter.)

This is why you can't call up a co-man and say, "I've been making this product in my kitchen, but I'm ready to scale up." The co-man will hang up on you because he will immediately think you're like the seaweed chip lady.

You see, an experienced co-man knows there's a high risk that they will put in a lot of work in for nothing. They get 20 calls a week from people who have a dream, but they also get calls from people who are already selling millions of dollars a year. So now you understand why they can't afford to waste a bunch of time on an "I Have a Dream" person—not when that time could've been spent with a company that has an existing product.

Getting Perspective
You think you're on your way to commercial production because you've been making six chocolate truffles per minute and selling them in a local storefront or at the farmers market, right?

Unfortunately, a co-man won't respect that level of production, even if it's a fast rate for the product you've been making.

It's important to understand that you can't call up a co-man and say something like, "I want to make this awesome sauce on a commercial scale, but I haven't done it on a large scale yet. It was my grandmother's recipe, and she's wonderful. Everybody likes it and says I should bottle it." If this is you, you need to scale it up yourself or get a research chef.

I can't tell you how many times I've heard that about sauces. I say, "Great, fantastic; what's the recipe?" And they have a recipe scribbled on an index card that makes enough for a family reunion, no more.

Then I ask, "Is it shelf stable?" And they say, "Oh, we can keep it for three days in our refrigerator."

Okay, well, here is the thing: Do you plan to sell it refrigerated? Do you plan to sell it shelf stable? They don't know what they don't know, so a lot of them can never find a co-man.

You need to try making it on an industrial scale in a commercial kitchen for a while and find out what you don't know. A research chef can be a good shortcut to take because they typically have some perspective in this area and could help you fill in the gaps. The only way to find out the answer to a lot of these questions is to make it yourself on a large scale until you've worked out every kink in the process.

This is the deal: Even small co-mans won't be interested until you have a couple hundred grand in sales. If you approach co-manufacturers before you've got some solid sales, any co-man that will take you on is bound to rob you. He's going to give you a horrible contract, and he is going to charge you every step of the way because he's minimizing his risks and covering his opportunity costs. After all, he is investing his time and resources in your untested operation that will most likely go under, when he could be investing in a company that might turn into the next Kellogg's.

In a nutshell, if you're an "I Have a Dream" person, the two things you need to do are:

- One, call an independent grocery store or someone like Whole Foods to try to get an appointment (so you can start selling your product somewhere).
- Two, find a commercial kitchen and start making your product *en masse* or at least on some sort of scale.

Then a co-man might take you seriously.

Remember: I'm not being a jerk by telling you the harsh truth. I'm just preventing you from burning bridges by contacting co-mans before you're properly prepared. Now, I'll help you understand what you need to do to overcome this obstacle. Basically, you need to start making your product somewhere other than your kitchen.

What is a Commercial Kitchen?
A commercial kitchen is a large kitchen that comes equipped with industrial-sized equipment like mixers, blenders, etc. You rent the room for a daily or weekly fee.

After you've paid your fees, you go and make your two pallets of sauce, your 200 jugs of coffee, or whatever. As you do this, you will work out what the process is to recreate Grandma's soup. Commercial kitchens are fantastic places to work out your recipes, production processes, and details regarding packaging and storage.

A lot of commercial kitchens have developed quality control programs to help you with the quality side, like how to keep things sterile and in compliance with health standards, which is something you need to learn. Keep in mind, they do this so they don't get sued, not so you don't, but this is still to your advantage. You will learn important things about production, storage, and packaging that you never would have known without having the actual experience.

In many cases, I can tell you where there's a commercial kitchen near you, so go ahead, shoot me an email at w.madden@right-brain-consulting.com and ask. If I know one near you, I'll let you know about it.

But Can't I Just Skip This Step?
Unfortunately, the answer is "No!" Unless you have $100,000 sitting around ready to invest, that is. And even if you *do* have the cash lying around, you will still benefit from at least one weekend in a commercial kitchen. So, if you really want to skip it, hire a research chef.

Why?
You need to make your product by yourself for a while because you need to decide if this is a business you love enough to get into, suffer through the growing pains of the first couple years, and then stick with long term, which is when you'll finally make a shit-ton of money. Then, when it does come time for you to find a contract manufacturer, you'll realize that it doesn't matter if it's a little bit more expensive than you expected, or a little bit cheaper—whatever the case ends up being. You won't care because you won't want to make it yourself anymore, and you'll understand why it costs what it does to hire a co-man or a co-packer to handle it for you.

I know it might sound intimidating at first. You may want to leapfrog over this step and try to find a cheap co-man, but I assure you, that sort of move will result in one of these two scenarios:

- A lot of rejection (because every co-man you approach will say no).
- A terrible contract with a co-man who robs you blind (because he's shoring up against the losses he assumes he will rack up).

An Example of What You'll Learn in the Commercial Kitchen

When you're working in the commercial kitchen, you should hire a research chef with manufacturing experience for at least one run. As you do this, you should start documenting all your manufacturing processes. You'll need this to prevent problems later on, problems that should have been identified and solved way back in the commercial kitchen phase of launching your business.

I watched a small company blow this piece of the puzzle once. I was sourcing a contract manufacturer for a frozen pizza company. This was a big project; I sourced over 20 co-mans and whittled them down to two. We were on the final tours; one co-man was huge, and the other was small. I stressed with my client the importance of going with the small company even though they were in love with the big one. They toured both plants and decided the big company was the way to go. We then started negotiating the contract, costing the company over $5,000 in just my fees. We dug out more than 20 very unfavorable clauses and got everything in place only to discover two weeks from launching the product that their wrapping machine did not go any larger then 12 inches, and they planned to put 15-inch pizzas into twist-tied bags.

The worst part was that they hadn't even told the company. I discovered it by doing a final check on the cost card, where instead of shrink film I saw a line labeled "trash bag". We then called the small company, who honored their original quote. We negotiated the contract, ordered materials, and were up and running in three weeks.

And in case you were wondering, the contract negotiations took less than a day and cost my client about $600. I got him out of that mess, which would have cost him in the tens of thousands of dollars had I not intervened.

The point? You'll learn a lot from the commercial kitchen experience. Once inside, you'll have access to industrial equipment and a boatload of knowledge from the people who work there.

Where Can I Find a Commercial Kitchen?
Commercial kitchens are sprouting up everywhere, but the Kitchen Coop (http://www.the-kitchen-coop.com/) is a good one in Denver that you'll want to check out. If you don't live in Denver, start Googling commercial kitchens in your area. Compare them to the Kitchen Coop; look for something similar in scale and service. Then book your first session and get ready to rock and roll.

Summary: Scaling Your Recipe
Between making product in your own kitchen and finding a co-man, you'll need to spend some time in a commercial kitchen and with a chef consultant. Find out what works, what doesn't, and whether you still have the passion for your product. The time you spend in the commercial kitchen will be so valuable that you'll wonder why you ever wanted to skip this step.

Chapter 4: Why You Need to Have the Finances Worked Out

This is one of the most important pieces of the puzzle. Money does indeed make the world go round, and it's essential for a food company, especially in the beginning stages.

Contract manufacturers are not charities. They are not doing this out of the goodness of their hearts. They're doing this to make money. You are doing this to make money.

The Co-Man's Primary Concern: Show Me the Money
The biggest problem with being in the food industry is capital. You will have to pay for everything in advance. You will have to wait at least 30 days to get your money from retailers after you've spent it, and you'll have to hold inventory, move inventory, and find buyers for that inventory.

You're going to need money—a *lot* of money. A lot more than you think you need. If you don't have $100,000 in capital to invest, you need to set your plans to find a co-man aside for a bit and first go figure out how you're going to get the cash. I've found that anyone with less than $100,000 to invest won't make it in this business, not on a commercial scale.

Why do you need so much money? Because you need to pay upfront for all the costs of the following:

- Production, including ingredients, line time, manpower, kitchen space, etc.
- Packaging, storing, and transporting the product.
- Marketing the product, including artwork and design.
- Slotting fees and promotions to get your product into stores.
- Travel, presentations, sales pitches.
- Brokering fees, accounting fees, business expenses.

All these things cost money.

You won't get money back until you sell the product, and it takes a while to establish yourself with retailers and in the market overall.

Be Realistic
Right now in this industry, you can feel your way to about a million dollars' worth of sales out of a commercial kitchen without help from someone like me who will hook you up with a good co-man. You should be able to do this over the course of three or four years. In that early phase of your start-up, you'll focus mostly on the practical aspects of how to make, package, store, and transport your product. You'll worry about selling it, too, but you'll still be working out your processes on the production side.

But after a million dollars, you will need to stop making your product and start concentrating on *selling* your product.

When you are at a million dollars in sales, you will not be making any money. You might have gross margins at 40% to 50%, and it should *look* like you're making money, but you won't be. With trade spend, broker fees, travel, plus all of the costs I listed above, you'll be lucky if you break even.

What I'm saying is this: You can probably get to the point where you're selling a million dollars worth of product, but you will also have spent at least a million dollars to make that happen.

And how will that happen? For most of you, you'll have raised money from your friends, your family, and your friends' cousins. You might have an angel investor or two that you know, but you're at a point where you need big money to grow quickly.

But how can you get the money you need? You'll want to look into the myriad of options currently available to see if you can raise the capital required to succeed.

Crowd-funding

Unless you've been living on a deserted island, you've heard about companies that have sprung up out of nowhere, supported by the contributions of the many. Crowd-funding, a method of fundraising that involves many people donating money either out of a sense of charity, purpose, or for a stake in the business, is becoming increasingly popular.

This is also a great way for food companies, like you, to get started.

The following are my two favorite crowd-funding sites:

1. Kickstarter (www.Kickstarter.com)

Smaller companies or individuals who want to try out a project often use this crowd-funding site. For example, you might sponsor an indie film production on LGBT rights, or you might sponsor someone who wants to print his first graphic novel. You'll probably get some small reward for your contribution, like a tee shirt or a bag of coffee beans, but really Kickstarter appeals to the charitable at heart—people who just want to support a "good cause."

If you want to succeed on Kickstarter, you'll want to appeal to the greater good or altruistic side of people by marketing your product launch as one of the following:

- Super duper good for you, providing a healthy alternative to some universally-denigrated junk food
- Charitable, as in a certain percentage of the profits will benefit a compelling, charitable cause
- Creative, appealing to some artistic segment of the population

It's a great idea to try out your project on Kickstarter before you go any further. See how much capital you can raise there, and then use that money to produce your product in a commercial kitchen and sell it on a small scale. Then see if you can get more support and funding.

Kickstarter is an ideal stepping-stone for anyone who isn't sure if they want to invest 100% into their project but know they want to give it a whirl.

2. CircleUp (www.circleup.com)
According to *Forbes* magazine, CircleUp has helped over 30 companies raise more than 30 million dollars in startup capital in two years' time (2012-2014). That's some serious cash.

This crowdfunding site has made a name for itself in the food industry in particular. Rhythm SuperFoods, which makes kale chips, and Bhaki Chai, a type of tea manufacturer, are just two of the many food companies that have gotten their business going thanks to CircleUp.

You'll want to check these guys out after you have a few hundred thousand in sales.

More Crowdfunding Sites
Unfortunately, this space is becoming crowded (no pun intended), with lots of teensy-weensy crowdfunding sites popping up everywhere, most of which are not successful or reliable. You'll want to use something proven (so you don't get burned).

The following are reputable crowdfunding sites that have been proven to be successful:

- IndieGoGo (https://www.indiegogo.com/)
- CrowdFunder.com (https://www.crowdfunder.com/)
- RocketHub (http://www.rockethub.com/)
- SomoLend (https://somolend.com/)

As you look into these, you'll discover that some of them cater to charitable contributors and some appeal to investors who want a stake in your business. Read the fine print carefully before you launch your first crowdfunding effort.

Business Incubators

Business incubators bring in an external management team to help you figure out how to launch your business, but we don't endorse any of them. They work out all the details with you, mentoring you as you go through the growing pains, usually for a fee or for a stake in your business. Business incubators ask for a much larger amount of equity in the business than accelerator programs, and they stick with the company for a much longer time.

A popular business incubator is IdeaLab (http://www.idealab.com/), located in Pasadena, CA. I'm not saying that you should use these guys, only that they are a primo example of a business incubator and one you should use as an example when looking for one to work with you. You can learn more about how these places work by visiting their websites.

Accelerator Programs

Some people refer to accelerator programs as business incubators on steroids. They are the latest and greatest of this sort of launching pad for small businesses. They work faster, produce more results in a shorter period of time, and require a smaller (financial) chunk of your success than business incubators. They're the crash course version of business incubators.

Accelerator programs differ from business incubators in that they ask for single-digit chunks of equity in your business in return for small amounts of capital and mentorship. They usually only work with a company for a three- to four-month program "boot-camp" style, from which your company will "graduate" after being set up for success.

31

My favorite accelerator program is AccelFoods (www.accelfoods.com). They work with emerging companies that are committed to changing the food industry. They offer engaged support to help packaged food and beverage entrepreneurs position themselves to scale. They do this through a hands-on team, seminars, and a community comprised of their mentors, strategic partners, and financial resources.

I'm a huge fan of accelerator programs because they are an affordable way to get the foundational pieces of the puzzle in place. I'd encourage you to find an accelerator program like AccelFoods that you think will be well suited to your business.

Another Personal Favorite
I work with a lot of marketing and business development specialists, but I've had better experiences with some than others. A lot of my clients have had positive experiences with HSR Associates (www.hsrassociates.net), a company that basically sets up your food business for you. They help you with your marketing, branding, packaging, etc. They also help you find your broker sales forces and explain the ins and outs of the business to you.

Summary: Test, Fund, Scale
It's a good idea, number one, to test your idea with a Kickstarter campaign.

Then, once you've raised your initial capital, make a batch in a commercial kitchen. Use the sales of the product you made in that first batch (or, more likely, several batches) to fund more production and promotion of your product, augmenting your funding with money contributed by friends and family.

Then, as you're slugging along, approach CircleUp or something similar, and see if you can get some major backing, some true venture capital.

But if you don't have $100,000, don't call quite yet. If you have less than that, get really comfortable with a commercial kitchen, make test batches, and get an appointment with some independent or all natural co-op grocery store. Make connections with independent stores that have one or two locations. Go out there and sell your product yourself for a while.

Of course, having money to invest makes the process easier, but you'll still have to work through the same problems as those who don't have money. You'll just have experts who know the industry helping you figure out your obstacles sooner.

If you don't have the capital yet, start in a commercial kitchen with a Kickstarter and build your way up from there.

Chapter 5: Problem - Nobody Thinks Your Product is Special (Except You)

I know you just finished reading the last two chapters and you're saying to yourself, "Oh my God, will I ever be able to do this? Please, sweet baby Jesus, let me just return this book."

Now that I've adequately discouraged you, I want to remind you that today is indeed the age of the new bright and shiny food business revolution, where all kinds of small companies are finding ways to make it big. Niche markets are flourishing, and products you never would have imagined would make it are flying off the shelves.

Think about it. Ten years ago, would you have predicted that KALE would become a thing? And yet there are all these (very popular) kale products on the market. Don't even get me started on bacon products. After decades of everyone saying bacon is this evil food that should never be consumed, the bacon revival has inspired everything from bacon-flavored lollipops to bacon-topped cupcakes.

Before we get into the details of what these little companies discovered (and what you need to figure out about your product before you get started), you will want to check out the following two-page spread documenting the evolution of the organic food industry in the past decade.

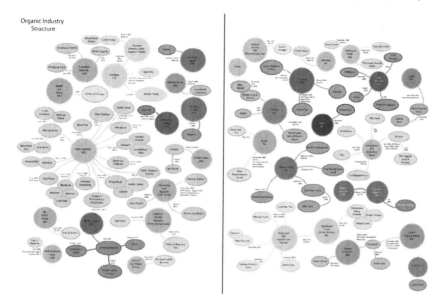

Organic Industry Structure

Starting a food company now is a lot different than starting a food company 10 years ago. Today people are starting food companies for the sole purpose of selling them in 5 or 10 years. If you're in the food business to create something to hand down for generations, this isn't the time. Most people are in this specifically to grow the company to the point where they can turn around and sell it. You will want to get to what's called "proof of concept" and then sell your little company to a bigger company.

But before you can do that, you need to sell a co-manufacturer on your product. To do that, you've got to identify and showcase your product's points of differentiation.

What Makes Your Product So Special?

You love your product; you think it's the best stuff in the world. The problem is, you need to prove to a co-manufacturer that your product is unique and marketable, and that requires numbers.

You need to be able to answer the following questions with real numbers and specific answers, backed with spreadsheets showing data:

- How much money have you made in sales thus far?
- How much product have you sold? To whom did you sell the product? What makes your product different from others similar to it?
- How can you prove there is sufficient demand for your product?
- Who is your target consumer for the product?

You won't want to say things like, "My product is unique and special because..."

- It tastes good.
- People like it.
- My family gobbles it up.
- It was a hit at the reunion. (This is the number one thing people say to me. That's why I keep mentioning it.)

You need proof that comes in the form of numbers from sales and market research results. Those results need to be compiled into compelling presentation materials that can be delivered to potential co-manufacturers and buyers with professional-looking graphs and summaries.

Think of your meetings with potential co-mans as sales presentations, because that's what they are. You are selling the co-man on your product, and part of that sales pitch is solid proof that your product is:

- Desired by a significant portion of the population.
- Can be (and has been) sold to that demographic.
- Different enough (and more appealing than) the existing products in its niche.

- Something that will become a popular item and result in repeat purchases.

Make sure you are prepared to sell the co-man on your product before you waste a phone call.

Summary: Prove That Your Product IS Special
Validate your claims that your product is worthy of investment via numbers from market research and sales records. Put those numbers into a Power Point presentation or impressive graphs that prove that your product really is the next superstar that will sweep the market.

Chapter 6: You Haven't Even Thought About Branding

What will set your product apart from all the others? When someone looks at your product on the shelf, how will they identify it? What will make them want to try your new product instead of another?

Do you know what branding is? Branding is the process of creating a unique name, logo, and image that distinguishes your product from all the rest. It's the difference between Coca-Cola and generic soda, or Bud Light and Newcastle. A brand is what tells the world what to expect when they purchase your product.

Why Branding Matters
An effective brand does more than help you find a product on a shelf full of competing products. If you brand your product well, you will tap into the emotions of potential buyers, creating an emotional connection between your product and the buyer.

How is that possible?

Think for a moment about your favorite car commercial. Upon what emotions does the commercial play? Your sense of adventure? Your desire for safety? Mystery? Intrigue?

Each car company has poured tens of millions of dollars into creating a specific emotional experience they hope to convey to potential buyers through their brand. They've spent money on market research to determine what demographic is most likely to buy each model of car they produce, and then to determine what emotional response they need to tap into inside the demographic.

Are they selling to young, single men in their 20s and 30s? More mature men in their 40s and 50s (who finally have some cash to spend and want to indulge themselves)? Outdoorsy nature lovers with a need to power through rough terrain? Soccer moms who are paranoid about child safety? Men who need to compensate for feeling small?

Once they've identified the desired emotional connection, they hire experts to determine how they can best evoke that emotional response through multimedia.

Developing Your Brand

You need to figure out the same elements for your brand. Are you going to produce your grandmother's spaghetti sauce recipe? Is your sauce gourmet sauce for special occasions, or is it the good old everyday sauce made for pasta night? Are you looking to evoke an emotional connection that says "elegant, sophisticated, and worth the extra money" or "warm, cozy, yummy, and cheap"?

Figure out who your intended audience is and what emotional experience you want them to have. Then determine how you'll convey that through a logo, messaging, colors, packaging, and so on.

The Psychology Behind Sales

Your brand is also what helps you overcome the biggest obstacles of all: selling all that product you've finally produced. I know you're just thinking about how to make a bunch of product right now, but what you really need to think about is how on earth you'll get that product on and off the shelves.

People love their money. They don't want to part with their money unless they believe they will get something great for it. Hence, loyalty to brands they know and love.

Here is why people buy brands: Most people have been burned by a product. Remember back when you were a kid, and you saw those ads for Sea Monkeys? They were supposed to be these really intelligent pets that would follow your flashlight and do your bidding, right?

But then you spent your hard-earned money on them, only to find out that they are nothing more than baby brine shrimp. They aren't smart. They aren't cute. They don't even have little smiling faces like in the ad, and they are NOT interactive pets. They are fish food.

People hate disappointment. They hate losing money. They like predictability, and they like feeling that they wisely spent their money to get products they love. That's why people develop loyalty to their favorite brands.

You need to brand your product in such a way that you can convince a large number of people to stop spending money on their favorite brand and try your brand instead.

Get an Expert Opinion
Talk to a marketing expert. Find out how and why your product is different than what's out there already.

Then write up a true value proposition, which is essentially a summary of why your product is superior to what's out there and why it will sell. Now cut that down to 5 sentences.

Brand Your Product
Come up with a company name, logo, and idea for packaging that helps people associate a feeling with your product.

What will you call yourself? Don't pick anything cute like your wife's, kid's, or dog's name. Your last name is also a bad idea. People tend to think of these companies as jokes.

My advice is to pick something that has a relationship with the product. Take Right Brain Consulting; I picked the name because it applies to the logical side of the brain, and all the services I provide are logical. My clients are normally very creative business people who need help with the manufacturing side of the business. It also is a name that sticks with you. If I had named the company Heather Inc. or Liam Inc., who would have taken me seriously? Nobody.

Get some help with this. Hire a designer for the logo. Get advice from people who know what they're talking about.

Summary: Think Branding

Are you ready to create your brand? Do you have any idea how to do that? If not, how will you convince a co-man that you are worth the risk?

You need to have a company name, logo and branding strategy outlined. You need to know how you're going to sell the product in a way that turns the co-man's head. You have to make him go, "Wow... even *I'd* want to try that product."

Chapter 7: Practical Matters—Storing and Transporting Product

One of the growing pains of starting a food business is the issue of keeping and moving your product in a safe, sanitary manner. These are the type of practical issues that many small companies don't consider until they are trying to cram 1,000 boxes of popsicles into their minivan in 95-degree weather. (Don't laugh, I know someone who did that. When she asked me what to do, I told her to make 3 trips.)

Storage Issues: When You Outgrow That Spare Bedroom
Thus far, you've probably just made enough product to sell at weekend farmers markets or at a local independent store. Maybe you sell online and you're keeping your product in a spare room in your house. Or perhaps you keep it stored in the garage next to your boat.

All that will change when you make your first commercial batch of product. After all, you probably won't have room in your house anymore. You can't stick it in a storage warehouse unless you're sure it is food-grade clean, free from insects, and insulated.

That means you need to think through where you will store all this product. To do this, you'll have to ask yourself what your particular product needs. Maybe if you have a frozen product, it should be in a frozen warehouse.

(Yes, that is sarcasm you detect. But trust me, I've seen it all. You don't even want to know where some people have stored their product.)

Why Your Co-Man Will Care About Storage
Your co-man will ask you what your storage plan is.
Why will he care? Because he doesn't want to store product for you. You take it somewhere else, and he collects his

money. Warehouses store product; contract manufacturers usually don't.

You need to have concrete answers, and you need to know what it will cost to use the appropriate solution.

Trains, Planes, and Automobiles—The Many Challenges of Moving Product

Transportation is a bigger problem than you probably ever imagined. Let me give you an example to illustrate why this is so.

Let's say you've always dreamed of making and selling specialty chocolates.

Now, chocolate is a unique product. During the entire transportation process, it has to be kept at a temperature of between 68 and 72 degrees. If you transport or store chocolate at any temperature outside of that range, you'll have problems.

I had a client once who put his chocolates in a frozen rather than a refrigerated storage facility. It was a fairly small order, only $25,000-$35,000 worth of product, but still, nothing to bat an eye at. He assumed this wouldn't be a problem—I mean, the chocolate wouldn't melt, right? It would just be a little colder than usual. He assumed it would still maintain its shape and appeal.

After the product was delivered to the retailers, he started getting calls that the chocolate was bad because it had become discolored. What happened? It had started a process called "blooming." That's when chocolate turns white. Have you ever bought an old chocolate bar? There's nothing wrong with it. It just looks "bad."

Often new business owners don't really understand their product or they don't grasp the nuances. Like, if you sell chocolate, just forget about selling it in the Southeast or Southwest during the summer. Just don't do it; people will offer to buy it, but even though you store it in a refrigerated facility, ship it in a refrigerated trailer, and insist that the distributors store it in a refrigerated facility, you will find out that somewhere between when you made it and the consumer got it, it melted or froze.

Side note for those who produce chocolate: Even if you manage to get the transportation piece right, you still need to be particularly careful in places with really high temps, you know, like Texas, where it's one hundred and fifteen degrees in the shade. The potential for disaster is simply too high. Let me explain why.

Everybody might have done everything right throughout the whole process until it got to the store, but these places have problems with keeping air temps stable. While H-E-B and Kroger have nice refrigerated storage areas, the corner market doesn't. The corner market is 1500 square feet and has 50 people an hour coming into it. There's a reason why store clerks all have fans on them. Your bars and margins will melt... and say hello to returns!

Yes, You, Too, Must Think About Transportation
Chocolate is not the only product that needs to be transported with care. Chips need to be transported in such a way that they don't get squashed, sandwiches need to remain cold, bottles of liquid (or sauce) need to be transported so they don't break. Really look at your product and think about it in a truck... then ask yourself: What could possibly happen?

You must also recognize that transportation can be very expensive. Your co-man might agree to make the product for you but then say, "And you've got to get this out of my plant by 3:00 p.m. on the day of production."
Some transportation issues to consider:

- How much room will your product require? What sort of trucks are equipped to move your product? Consider size, volume, special conditions, etc.
- Where does your product need to go? Multiple sites? One site?
- How far away does your product need to go?
- How much will it cost to move your product?
- What sorts of transportation tariffs might you be required to pay?

Make sure you've thought through all the details and contacted potential transportation companies to get estimates.

Figuring Out Transportation

After you know what special arrangements you need for transportation and storage, talk to the co-man about it. You should always ask if he could offer storage at a cost. If he can't handle your requirements, ask if they have a relationship with a "3PL" and ask if you can piggyback their rates. If they agree, then your storage rate per pallet will be the same as theirs. (In case you don't know what 3PL means, it means "third party logistics." If you say 3PL, they might think you know what you're talking about. And remember, you want to sound like you know what you're talking about as much as is possible.)

Overcoming the Transportation Obstacle

As you figure out things like how your product will get to the store, and who will store your inventory, you'll hit snags or find out that some of these parts of the process can be very expensive. You'll need to figure out what will be the best deal for you. For example, will you distribute using a distributor or by selling through the customer's warehouse?

When you explore options, you'll find out that most of your distributors are not willing to come get your product. Most of them will say, "I'd like this product delivered to me."

Unfortunately, you're new on the scene, and you're transporting a relatively small amount of product compared to your competitors, so you are not a power-buyer when it comes to negotiating transportation costs. You're a cost-taker. Remember: No one gives a shit about your business, and nobody cares about the $50,000 a year that you spend in transportation costs.

What you want to do is look for opportunities to take advantage of something called pickup allowances.

What you do is this: You go to your customers and say, "I will give you a dollar a case or $1.50 a case to pick up." That might be half of what it costs for you to ship. Unfi (United Natural Foods Inc.) and Kroger are two of the greatest advocates of backhauling. They have trucks all over the country all the time. If you get to work with these companies, always propose backhaul arrangements to them. It's dirt cheap for them to do a backhaul since they have their own trucks. They deliver to a grocery store full and then return empty. If they make an arrangement with you, they can pick up your product and return full. There is little to no additional cost for them to backhaul your product. So arrange pick up allowances whenever possible because 90% of the time it will be cheaper than you shipping it.

Summary: Know Your (Storage and Transportation) Plans
You'll need to find out the answers to all these questions before you approach a co-man. Be ready with concrete answers, likes names and numbers of the companies who will transport and store your product, should the co-man agree to work with you.

Chapter 8: You Have No Clue How Your Product Should Be Packaged

Have you ever bought an Apple product? Did you notice how your new iPhone was packaged in branded, beautifully wrapped packaging that was perfectly fitted to the device? Likewise, you need to think through the details of how packaging will best showcase your product.

In a nutshell, your packaging needs to be:

- Aesthetically pleasing (it needs to look good).
- Practical (so you don't have a mess).
- Inexpensive (because otherwise you'll lose all your profits to packaging).

You'll want to think through all of these factors so you know exactly what you want when you finally speak to a co-man. They will expect you to know what you want.

When the co-man asks you how you want it packaged, you do not want to be stuck on the phone, stuttering something like, "Uh... I don't know. What do you recommend for packaging?"

You need to have a good idea of what you need before you get on the phone.

Appearance Matters

Some people want to use the packaging as part of their sales tactic, their shtick, if you will. You know, like biodegradable packaging for packs of chips, or all recyclable materials. You should do this; it will require you to think through how your packaging will work with your branding. For example, if your branding is all natural and eco-friendly, you won't want to package your product in Styrofoam and a plastic bag.

You will also want to think about what kind of packaging will appeal most to your demographic. You'll want to hire a designer to help you figure out things like color, logo, labeling, and what looks good. Ask questions like:

- What type of packaging will present my product in the most appealing way? Cardboard box? Plastic cup? Glass bottle? Jar?
- What sort of labeling will be most attractive? What colors should I use, and what sorts of images and fonts should I employ?
- Will I need layers of packaging, like sealed plastic bags inside a cardboard box?

Don't trust your own judgment; talk to someone in the business who knows about packaging options and aesthetics.

Packaging That Makes Sense
You will also need to think about what your product needs for practical purposes. For example, how can you safely stack your product when transporting it in bulk? What sort of packaging will keep your product intact so it looks good when opened by the consumer? Will your product be shelf-stable? Is there a type of packaging that can extend the shelf life?

If your product is refrigerated or frozen, you need to think through issues like temperature variances and heating options. Do you want your product to be packaged in such a way that it can withstand both heat and cold, like those packets of steamable vegetables you buy in the frozen section of the supermarket, but cook in the bag in your microwave?

Figure out how practicality needs to factor into your packaging choices.

Money, Money, Money
As you make packaging decisions, you will also need to evaluate how your packaging choices will affect your costs.

Let's take pouch packages as an example. A film impression of roll stock might cost you about eight cents per impression whereas preformed bags cost about 14 cents per unit. And preformed bags are filled by hand, whereas roll-stock pouch packages are auto-filled, so the associated labor costs are also higher for preformed bags.

You will need to consider the following costs:

- How much the actual packaging costs.
- How much any special effects or designs will cost (e.g., the more colors, the higher the price).
- How much the equipment for or process of packaging will cost you.
- How much of your profit margin you are willing to sacrifice for the luxury of a certain type of packaging.
- How hard it will be to fill.

You may need to delay some options for the future, after you are established. For example, if you're just starting out, you'll want to avoid costly packaging like zipper bags, because the equipment that makes zipper bags is very expensive and is completely different from the equipment that makes pouch packages. While consumers like zipper bags, they come with a pretty significant cost. However, you could use pouch packages for the first year, and then plan to upgrade to zipper bags later.

Summary: Know What You Want and What You Can Afford

You need to already have an idea of what materials you want to use, how much you can spend, and how the packaging will fit into the process overall.

Will you ask the co-man for packaging options, or will you work with a separate co-packer? How will the packaging fit into the production and distribution cycle? You can't approach co-mans or co-packers until you have an idea of what you want and can afford.

Chapter 9: You Don't Know What Regulations Apply

You need to learn what government regulations apply to your product. For example, you will need to provide a full ingredient and nutritional statement. But do you know if the USDA regulates your product? Do you know how to determine your shelf life? Have you done a hazard analysis? Do you know what allergens are in the product? What are the government requirements for production, storage, packaging, transportation, and selling? What do you need to do in case of a recall?

If you don't know the answers to these questions, a co-man will have nothing to do with you. The co-man won't be willing to take on your liability.

While writing this, I tried to think of a story I'd have to tell you, a good warning story. Because this is serious stuff. But guess what? I've dodged this bullet with all my clients. I've made sure my clients don't screw up in this area, because I realize how huge of a deal this is.

Claims and standards of identity are some of the most confusing laws with which to comply. I highly recommend that any claim be reviewed by a labeling attorney. Labeling firms will review all the information and research to ensure you stay out of court. You need to connect with a lawyer who will:
- Evaluate your product
- Let you know what should concern you, and
- Help you take the necessary actions to protect yourself against lawsuits.

Start paying attention to the news about recalls and truth in advertising lawsuits. Just recently Red Bull was subjected to a $13M verdict. Why? Because they claimed Red Bull gives you wings. Who the hell really believed you would grow wings like a cartoon?

Watch Your Claims

If you say your product is going to help you to lose X percentage of weight, you'd better have clinical trials that prove that people lose X percentage of weight. If you say it's gluten-free, you'd better have proof that it's gluten-free. Do not wind up in a truth-in-labeling claim suit. Please note that all those symbols you see on packages are certifications. It is important that you realize that you cannot put those seals on your packages unless you go through the appropriate processes.

Label Accurately

Make sure you list all your ingredients in the correct order. Make sure you list all of your allergens. Find out what warnings (e.g., manufactured in a plant that also processes peanuts) should be included on the label, and what is acceptable or unacceptable. Is it okay to list "spices" instead of listing out every spice you used? What if your spice mix contains MSG? Do you need to include that in the list? Your contract manufacturer should provide guidance when it comes to allergens, but not when it comes to claims.

Find out if you will need to explain certain ingredients (like breaking down active versus inactive ingredients, or explaining what an ingredient is, such as an emollient or preservative) on the label. You might not think these are important details, but the government will.

Research Safety Issues

Does your product run the risk of triggering an allergic reaction? Will it go bad after four months on the shelf? Does it need to be consumed within X number of days of being opened? How long will it stay fresh in the refrigerator?

You will need to get a professional assessment of the safety issues surrounding your product. You probably don't know all the possible safety issues, so get an expert involved. Your co-man should help you find a lab to conduct shelf life testing. DO NOT SKIP THIS STEP.

Learn How to Talk Label-Speak

It's one thing to find out your product may cause epileptic seizures or go bad in four days; it's another thing to know how to communicate this information in the proper format on a label. You don't want to sound like the side effects list on a pharmaceutical product, but you also don't want to sound like a dolt. Get advice on how to properly label your product so you avoid sounding like your product is a health time bomb while still avoiding a lawsuit.

Regulation Basics

The first thing you need to determine is this: Is the item USDA?

This is easy: If it has meat in it (at all), it is USDA. If it doesn't, it is FDA. You need to know this because all the labels must be reviewed by the correct governmental agency. There are some loopholes for sandwiches, but just to be safe, call the USDA office and ask.

Technically, everything is regulated by the FDA, but the FDA defers to the USDA when an item falls into the USDA's guidelines. Your co-man will help you with any USDA submissions you need to make. They are rather complicated, so listen to your co-man—they can submit, but have your lawyer review the submission beforehand.

Hire Someone to Verify Claims or Run Trials

You have to have the claims verified in order to show that you've done due diligence. So if you say it's organic, it's got to have an organic cert. If you say it's sugar-free, you have to be able to prove that it's sugar-free.

You have to be able to prove these things in case anybody ever questions them. For example, if you say there are three ounces of product in a box, the box needs to contain three ounces (or more). Otherwise you have a problem with what's called weights and measures. The government goes out and periodically checks products to see if they're underweight. And if it is underweight, they fine you, fine the store, and then make you pick up the product. Plus the store will ask you to provide details to prove you meet the MAV (Maximum Allowable Variation). And don't think the store will pay that fine or the costs to pull the product. That will all be on you.

Understanding the Implications of Recalls
Now imagine that happens. Let's say you have product on the shelves in 1,100 Kroger stores. You then take back 1,100 Kroger stores' worth of product. Product in the field gets destroyed, because it doesn't pay to have it packed back up and sent to you. Product in the warehouse gets returned, and the store takes an immediate credit against open invoices. The real kicker is that they won't buy from you again until you can prove that the issue has been resolved or that it was a one-off.

Chances are, that store chain won't *ever* buy from you again. I mean, you're not a big boy yet—you're not Purdue or Kellogg's, so they won't take a risk with you again. The risk of another recall is not worth it to them.

How A Recall Will Affect You Financially
I'm going to paint a picture for you so you'll understand how serious a recall is. Keep in mind, I'm just running general numbers. I'm not taking into account every expense, but this will help you get the point.

Let's say you sold your product at $10/case.

You bought it at $5/case.

Ten thousand cases have been returned (due to the recall), so you pay out $100,000. You only get credit for $50,000.

Your cash flow takes a $50,000 hit.

Plus you're off the shelves for a month, costing you $50,000 in sales.

You buy new product from the co-man with 15-day terms, which means you need to move cash to pay the co-man because stores buy from you with 30+ day terms.

Do you have the money to absorb a situation like this? Hopefully you now understand why a recall is such a big deal.

Protecting Yourself

USDA items are the food products that are under the most scrutiny. If you've got a USDA product, you need expert help to protect your ass. There's no way around this.

First, you have to submit your ingredient statements, your labels, all of that, to the USDA. Have your lawyer review these submissions before your co-man sends them in. Every submission and their corrections can take up to 12 weeks to get reviewed, so do it right the first time. AND NEVER, EVER market a USDA item that has not been approved. You will be lucky if they only fine you and make you recall the product. The USDA is no joke. IF they say something just do it; do not argue. When it comes to food and manufacturing plants, they are as close to God as you can get.

Plan on them checking what's called standard of identity, which is basically certifying that the stuff you say is in the product really is what you say it is. For example, if you're selling New Zealand lamb meatballs, 50% of the meat has to come from New Zealand and has to be lamb. If you are selling a brick oven pizza, it had better be made in a brick oven.

Your co-man is supposed to stay current and make sure his facility is in compliance, not that *your* claims are. So while your co-man can advise you on your claims, you really need expert advice from a lawyer about this piece of the puzzle. Your co-man's advice is just the starting point when it comes to claims.

If you're in a good commercial kitchen, they might help you with submittals as well, but you have to make sure it is a certified USDA facility. One thing you never, ever, ever want to do is put an USDA item out there that's not made in a USDA facility. The government will fine you, and you'll most likely be accused of producing a health hazard because it wasn't made to the USDA's standards. And if your product hurts someone, you will go to big boy jail.

FDA standards are also important to meet, but USDA standards are the most important. They are very stringent, and you must follow their procedures and get certifications in the proper manner or risk serious consequences.

Summary: Compliance is Something You Can't Ignore
Don't make the mistake of sweeping compliance issues under the rug. Yes, they're a pain in the ass. Co-mans realize how serious compliance issues are. If you act like they aren't important, you'll expose yourself as ignorant and unreliable. Don't burn bridges by making this fatal mistake.

Chapter 10: You Don't Have a Business Plan or Proof You Are Ready to Scale

Remember that lemonade stand you ran outside your house as a kid?

You used your parents' lemonade mix, and your indulgent neighbors paid you 50 cents a cup for your watered-down lemonade. They patted you on the head and commented on what a promising entrepreneur you were. You made a whole $8, which you promptly spent on junk from the dollar store or somebody's garage sale. Nobody even remembers what they bought with their "profits."

As an adult, you now see what happened.

Mom and Dad paid for your supplies.

Your neighbors bought your product to be nice to you. Your "sales" were in actuality acts of charity.

Believe it or not, you've probably been experiencing an adult version of the lemonade stand with your product.

The Adult Version of the Lemonade Stand
If you've just been making your product at home and selling it at farmers markets or online to friends and family, you probably:

- Have no idea how much this is really costing you.
- Have not had to deal with large-scale packaging, storing, transportation, sales brokering or recall costs.
- Have gotten a lot of pity sales from friends and family, who will always tell you that your product is awesome (even if it's not).

You've also not had to deal with all the basic running-a-business expenses. You know, things like:

- The time spent on accounting, record keeping, paperwork, tracking your product and sales, finding places to sell your product, researching compliance issues, making sure you have crossed all your 'T's and dotted all your 'I's, etc.
- The actual costs of buying raw materials and paying for production, packaging, transportation, getting shelf space in a store, etc.
- How to market your product to people who don't know you and who have no reason to consider your product.

Because you haven't had to deal with the impersonal, cutthroat market, you probably are not prepared for what this monster will really cost you. It's likely that you are not prepared (financially or emotionally) for the amount of time and investment it takes to successfully launch a business.

This is especially true if the only materials you've read so far are hyped up get-rich-quick business books and online materials. You know, the type of programs that promise to teach you how to launch a successful business for $99.99.

What You Need: A Well Thought Out Business Plan
You need a professional business plan, complete with numbers from your past efforts, predictions that have been verified by experts, and records of your experiences in the commercial kitchen. Add to this proof of funding, a financial plan (projecting out a minimum of one year), and a marketing plan.

You need to figure out things like what your profit margins are and how much you will need to use to reinvest in the business.

This is a point you need to consider carefully. Do you realize how much of your profits will need to go back into promoting your business? Rule of thumb is, 20% of your sales will go for trade spend alone, and that is only one part of promoting your business.

Let's talk about this one very important piece of the puzzle for a moment. Before I mentioned the phrase "trade spend," did you know what it was? Trade spend is the amount you need to spend for slotting or placement in a store and promoting it through discounts. It often shows up as the promotional fees paid to a retailer to get your product on the shelf or to distribute the product to the customer. Trade spend is just one aspect of running a food business that you have to understand and factor into your business plan if you want to succeed. That's why you see discounts in the store, where the normal price is $5.99 and it's on sale for $4.99. A lot of times that dollar off comes directly from you. So you pay those kinds of fees, and they amount to about 20% of your sales. Sometimes retailers will match your margin hit, but don't count on it.

I won't go into the details about this. Instead I'll advise you to buy a reputable book about business plans because this book is primarily about how to source a contract manufacturer, not how to start a business. However, you will need to learn how to wisely start a business if you want a co-man to take you seriously. Make sense?

Why You Need a Business Plan
You need a business plan for several reasons. One, you need to make sure you understand all the costs involved in launching or expanding your business. That may seem obvious to you, but it isn't obvious to a lot of people— especially entrepreneurs who are so excited about moving forward that they skip the planning phase.

The second reason you need a business plan is to convince a potential co-man that you are a solid partner.

I know you just want to find a co-man who buys into your dream, but you have to ask yourself: "Why would they invest in my business?"

If they bought into every dream, they would be out of business. Start-ups are risky, just by nature. The US Bureau of Labor Statistics <u>reports</u> that half of start-ups fail in the first five years of business, and the <u>University of Tennessee's Small Business Development Center of Research</u> tells us that the food industry has one of the highest failure rates of all the industries they track.

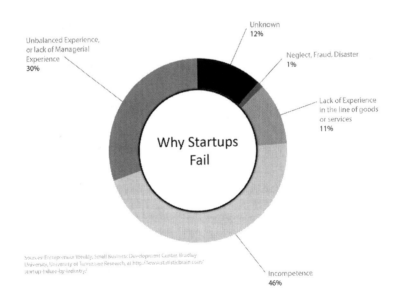

Unknown
12%

Unbalanced Experience, or lack of Managerial Experience
30%

Neglect, Fraud, Disaster
1%

Lack of Experience in the line of goods or services
11%

Why Startups Fail

Sources: Entrepreneur Weekly, Small Business Development Center, Bradley University, University of Tennessee Research, at http://www.statisticbrain.com/startup-failure-by-industry/

Incompetence
46%

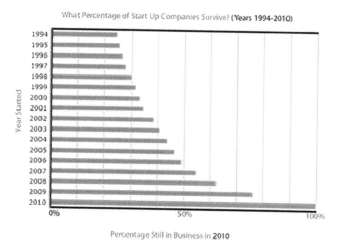

What Percentage of Start Up Companies Survive? **(Years 1994-2010)**

Percentage Still in Business in **2010**

Source: http://www.bls.gov/bdm/entrepreneurship/bdm_chart3.htm

The vast majority of people who have the dream of running a food company fail. If you were a co-man, would you take the risk of making product for a company that may soon be out of business, leaving you holding thousands of dollars in product and raw materials?

What I am trying to say is this: Don't waste their time or yours trying to sell them on the dream. They don't care; it's not their company. You have to prove that you are worthy of the risk, and that will require a respectable business plan that can be easily shared with a potential co-man.

Choose a book on business plans that forces you to drill down into all the details of starting your business, and projects what you need to invest and what it will take. If that book doesn't cover every area I've mentioned in this book, drop it and find something better.

Pretend that you will have to defend your business in a court of law. Prepare yourself with Excel spreadsheets of data, with graphs and diagrams. Detail your estimated costs and income, all that good stuff. Prepare a balance sheet.

Of course, if you hook up with an accelerator program or business incubator, they'll help you with all of this. If you're not sure you can tackle this piece of the puzzle on your own, hire someone to help you.

Proof You Are Ready to Scale

Along with a solid business plan, you also need to demonstrate that you have an understanding of what it takes to make the product in a manufacturing setting. Remember that the co-man has to make this product in a rapid, continuous process or they will never make money. They aren't sitting around in an industrial kitchen cooking up a batch of Grandma's spaghetti sauce just for fun.

As I mentioned in a previous chapter, to do this, you will need to have made the product in a commercial kitchen and employed a commercial chef for (at minimum) a consultation or (much better) at least one or two batches so you can learn from the chef. You will also need to be prepared to sell the large quantities of your product that the co-man will make, and you need to prove you have a plan for this.

How Do You Prove You Are Ready to Scale?

I have a client right now who's right around the million-dollar mark in product sales. When he started, he was producing at a rate of 6 pieces per minute. By the time he came to me, they were up to 70 pieces per minute.

Keep in mind that the technology that most co-mans would use produces at a rate of 350-500 pieces a minute.

But my client did this by hand, and as a result, his costs were completely out of control. At a rate of 70 PPM, you can imagine how high his internal costs were. His production rate was about 20% more than what a co-man's rate was.

As you can imagine, it was hard to find a co-man to work with him.

He had some of the work done—after all, he already had developed a recipe that was appropriate for contract manufacturing. However, I had to explain to him that a co-man would make this between 5 and 14 times faster than he was making it. I described how they would have giant mixers and would use a continuous process, so he had to be sure that he was ready for the jump in the amount of product he would have on hand and would have to sell.

So instead of making 10,000 lbs. a week, you're going to make 10,000 lbs in a day. You don't have an issue with scalability in the manufacturing end because the co-man is taking care of that for you. But you need to make sure that you'll be able to sell enough product to keep up with how quickly this equipment produces it.

This particular client produced in a factory with about 20 people, made it himself, chugging along, but he didn't have the internal capacity to really grow the business. When he came to me, he said, "I am looking for someone who can just make the hell out of this product." So that's what I found him.

Now, it was a little nerve-wracking when he said, "Oh my god, that's two weeks' worth of production that just happened in one running day." But it removed what was (at the time) his biggest handcuff—the "I couldn't make the product fast enough" problem. He was ready to scale his sales, so it all worked out.

Preparing to Scale: Get Your Pricing Set
One of the most important steps in preparing to scale is figuring out how and where you will sell product. This is more involved than you may think. You already know you need to approach stores about selling your product, but what do you need to do so it will get off the shelf and into consumers' homes?

As you line up stores for selling your product, you need to account for the following factors:

- Market pricing. (Price it so it'll sell!)
- What margin you need to make—your bottom line.
- The fact that you'll probably take a loss this first year or two while your brand gets established.
- How much you need to make to keep the lights on.
- Promotional strategy.
- Investor growth targets.

The other thing for which you need to prepare is what's called a free-fill or rack-share program, which is when you give the buyer the first order for free. Let's say I have 100 stores, and the clients put a case of your product in each store; you're giving me 100 free cases. If this is something you don't want to do, keep in mind there are 100 start-ups behind you who will. Remember trade-spend? Well, this is part of it.

So why do you need to give away free product?

When they take your product, you're taking that slot in the store from somebody else. A good example is when Lean Cuisine replaces Healthy Choice. All that Healthy Choice on the shelf gets discounted to move it out.

You give them a free case because number one, you're buying that shelf-space from them so they can afford to discount the product that was in the slot before you. And number two, it's a profit center for them, and it helps offset the cost of when they need to put in new fixtures or open new stores.

This is how you get your product out there so someone can actually have a chance to see it and buy it. The idea is that once it's out there and on that shelf, they're going sell it and then re-order from you at full price.

You also will have to factor in promotion pricing—this is when you sell product at a discount in order to build up a sales base. So when designing your model for how much money you're making, plan that you're going to have to invest 20% to give back to your retailer as free fills and promotional product. That is why your food is so expensive at retail. Keep in mind: even after all this money you give them, retailers typically only clear 1% or 2% profit a year. That's why investing in trade spend is crucial for your relationships with retailers.

Act Like this Isn't Your First Touchdown

You will want to do the legwork of talking to potential buyers before you approach a co-man about actually making your product. Then, when you talk to the co-man, it will be obvious that you have a plan to move product. You'll be able to say you have stores lined up and a sales plan in place. The only thing you'll still need is an excellent co-man to start making your product for you.

Summary: Will It Work For You?

You need to review your sales plan and determine what you will do with your increased product supply. I'm always astonished at how many small companies are so focused on getting more product made that they forget to figure out how the hell they will market and sell the product after it has been made.

Make sure you've thought this through and gotten some solid leads on places that will sell your product and a plan for financing the marketing and placement of product before you approach a co-man. You'll need to be able to prove you're able to handle the output before you can convince anyone to work with you.

Part III: Companies Already Manufacturing on a Commercial Scale

Earlier in the book I described three types of people who approach me for help finding a co-man. This chapter is for the third type of person I described.

Entrepreneur #3: A person who is already manufacturing the product and realizes that this is a huge distraction and financial suck.

You've done commercial kitchens and decided, "All right, it's time to hire a manufacturer." Perhaps you have a small factory going, and you've been employing people to make product for a while. You've moved a significant amount of product on your own, and you've got $100,000 to invest.

If you are this third type of entrepreneur, you will have a much easier time finding a contract manufacturer than the other people who read this book. You are a proven commodity, and contract manufacturers love proven commodities.

Unfortunately, you still are in a dangerous spot. Why? Because you face the following challenge: **The Size Match**

Understanding Why Size Matching Matters

It's as simple as this: Whenever possible, use a contract manufacturer the same size as you. You can grow together, you can manage cash flow together, and you will most likely be partners indefinitely.

I want to encourage you to slow down and make a careful decision. You've worked hard to get where you are right now.

I know you will probably be tempted to take whatever co-man is willing to work with you, especially if you don't have someone negotiating your contracts and helping you figure out which co-man would be a good fit for your company. After you've made 15 calls and had 15 doors slammed in your face, you'll think, "Oh, thank goodness someone wants to work with me!" You probably won't even know how to tell how big they are or if they are right for you unless you know what types of questions to ask.

I know you're tired of the commercial kitchen. I know you're sick of dealing with packaging and transportation. You've worked hard to get where you are right now; don't throw it all away because you're tired. Hang in there a little longer and set yourself up for long-term success.

The next two chapters explain why size matching is so important. Read on and learn what questions to ask and how to figure out if a co-man is the right (or wrong) size for you.

Chapter 11: Small Company Working With Large Manufacturer

Little companies usually like the idea of working with big companies. They think these big companies will be able to support their growth and give them the resources they need. Big companies talk about exciting-sounding things like product development support, purchasing power, market insights, and commercialization managers. All this sounds impressive and is meant to lull you into a sense of security... so that you will sign a contract that is definitely *not* to your advantage.

It's important to understand that, assuming you are a small company, none of these impressive-sounding promises will help you. Product development will always come at a cost, and often the manufacturer will retain ownership of the formula so you are locked in (and can never move to a new manufacturer). Their buying power always benefits them. They get rebates or extended terms as a way to generate revenue or create cash flow.

As a small company working with a large manufacturer, you have a couple pluses and a lot of minuses.

The pluses are: In theory, you don't have to worry about capacity anymore because you have a co-man that is big enough to make whatever the hell you want. That problem's solved.

A larger contract manufacturer also tends to be a lot more financially stable than a small contract manufacturer. They have huge institutional investors who have poured a lot of money into ensuring the co-man is well established.

They also have a stable of specialized resources to work with such as a well-trained staff that knows your segment of the industry.

They should have all of the necessary certifications such as: organic, Kosher, GFSI, etc.

The downside is... Well, there are several downsides to this matchup.

Blend together busting the myths and downsides. They seem sort of redundant.

Downside #1
You'd better figure out how to sell a ton of chocolate (or whatever it is your product happens to be). Because when you go to produce, you're producing 400,000 of something, not 25,000 of something.

Downside #2
The amount you're paying to the contract manufacturer is much higher than it needs to be, because they're ripping your ass off. They can charge you higher prices because they figure you've got nowhere else to go, and your business is a tiny fraction of their revenue. You are a small fish in a huge ocean.

Downside #3
They don't give a flying shit about your business. They don't care if you're there in the morning and gone in the afternoon. You're the last guy for whom they'll produce (because you're probably the smallest company with whom they're working), so they'll bump you from the schedule all day long. So they have the ability, not capacity.

You don't like it? What are you going to do? Go cry to your mommy? Leave them? They'll say, "Fine. Get lost. But you owe me this ridiculous amount of money for breaking the contract." You'll end up stuck with them, hoping they get around to making your product somewhere close to the agreed-upon schedule.

Downside #4

They're going to wake up one day and say, "We need to make more money, so we'll arbitrarily raise the price despite a contract with you. Why? Because we can." And how can they do this to you? Because they're thinking, "You'll go out of business if you don't go along with it, so you won't be around to sue us."

And it's true. Most of you are investing your every last penny into this venture. You don't have money for a lawsuit and all that garbage. So you'll pay the higher prices, just to stay in business. The ironic thing is, you might not be able to stay in business long, because those higher prices will eat up your margins, which means you'll have less money to invest into promoting your project. And without adequate product promotion, you'll never grow.

Downside #5

You're going to see an increase in your costs. They will always order your unique ingredients in the smallest quantities possible, and this will generally increase, not decrease, your costs.

Downside #6

Their market insights are usually out of date. After all, why do they care about the trends except for figuring out what they can make most cheaply (and easily) and then tailoring the numbers to reflect those products as the best new item? They'll tell you to make product that benefits them, not you.

Downside #7

You aren't high priority.

Because you are one of their smallest clients, you are the last on the list with which they share whatever market insight information they *do* have. They share it with companies who are their size first, and then give them the opportunities to get a head start on developing the new product. After all, they make their money by making product. And big companies sell a lot of product. You, my friend, do not sell a lot of product, so you get the information and attention last... if they have any time left for you.

Downside #8
Their commercialization managers will not look out for you.

Yeah, yeah... you'll get a commercialization manager assigned to you, but these are the most overworked guys in the company, often managing 70 or more projects at a time. They prioritize work like everyone else in the world does, so they work on the big projects first. I have a dozen or so horror stories of companies never getting their line extensions launched simply because the company could not get around to moving the project forward.

Downside #9
And finally pricing. Big companies don't need the smaller company's business, so they tend to raise their prices at will and have the attitude of "Good luck finding a new manufacturer before my increases go into effect."

I had one client who was actually told by a CEO that they were raising their tolling by 46% with less than 30 days' notice. When the smaller company's CEO said that would put them out of business, the co-man's reply was, "Oh, well. That's your problem."

It took the company over six months to find a new contract manufacturer and get out. Do you have that kind of cash just lying around? I didn't think so. And, by the way, when they left, the big company sued them for breaching the contract. Can you believe that bullshit?

Summary: In General, Big Co-Mans Abuse Little Companies

I've seen all of this and more happen. Big co-mans with little companies are big problems. Protect yourself from this sort of situation by asking about production numbers.

Now that I have said all this, I will admit that I do represent a few little companies that I have paired with big contract manufacturers. However, I also have huge clients with those co-mans, and those relationships eliminate any bullshit they might try. They know that if they screw with me on the little guy, I will really screw them on the big one. Also, if I move one company I can move all three.

I make these matches strategically, with good reason, and only with proper "insurance" in place.

Chapter 12: Larger Company Using Smaller Contract Manufacturer

I work hard to find the match that's exactly the right size for my clients because I understand how important this factor is. I'll go out on a limb here and bet that until reading this book, you never even thought about size-matching with a co-man. You just wanted to find somebody—anybody—to manufacture your product at a decent price for you.

I pointed this out because this is a very important part of the arrangement, and yet most people who come to me have never even thought about it.

On rare occasions, the size match doesn't matter, but those situations are unusual. I do have one "big" co-man against whom I've never heard a bad word. I've put two or three smaller companies in there, and no one's complained. They've jumped through hoops for each of the companies I've referred to them; they're a fantastic manufacturer. But if you're not going to buy 400,000 or 500,000 bars at a time, they're not the guy for you.

If you need to order 25,000 bars, I know another co-man who is a good guy for you. You'll pay through the nose, but they're a small, flexible company with a solid foundation. They can make 1,000 bars or they can make 25,000 bars; it is up to you.

The bottom line is this: You need to find a co-man who is the right size match for your company, and going with a manufacturer that is a lot bigger or smaller than you will most likely be a mistake.

You already know (from the last chapter) why you don't want to partner up with a co-man who is lot bigger than you, but you also need to understand what can happen if you go with a co-man that is too small.

Another Mismatch: Large Food Company, Small Co-Man
Larger companies using smaller contract manufacturers have their own set of problems.

You may think you're being smart, going with a small co-man and all. You're thinking things like, "We'll get personalized attention," and, "It's going to be all cozy."

And there *are* some benefits. Their pricing is normally wonderful because of their low overhead structure. You will generally have the personal contact information for your account manager and the owner. When you say, "Jump," their answer will be, "How high?" They will work day and night to get you what you need. All because they know that without you they will go out of business.

But there are several downsides to this matchup, all of which are important to consider.

Downside #1
You're going to get stuck paying for materials and equipment you normally wouldn't even have to consider, just to make sure your co-man can produce your product on time and as promised.

Unfortunately, smaller co-mans do not have the resources to handle the volume from a large company. They are a small company and will always be short on cash. God forbid you ever pay an invoice late; they can't make ends meet without you. There will be no room for mistakes, no space for a late payment on ANYTHING.

Their equipment is often old, outdated, and/or in general disrepair. But since you entrusted them to make your product, you'll find yourself paying for equipment repairs, replacement or else get stuck looking for another co-man long before you wanted to make the switch.

Once you figure out that your co-man NEEDS your business for their survival, you'll realize how tenuous the arrangement is.

Downside #2
Smaller plants are often older and have inadequate quality systems or certifications. You can get in big trouble with the government if they are out of compliance. Some of them have been flying under the radar for years, but now that you are there, all eyes are on them. When the shit hits the fan for this, you're the one who gets covered in doo-doo.

Downside #3
The further along in the relationship you get, the more you'll find out where they've been cutting corners and how vulnerable this makes you. Maybe they're buying cheap ingredients, or skimping on quality control. They're just barely surviving, so they're doing what they have to do to get by, and you will end up sharing the liability with them.

Let's say your little co-man screws something up with sanitation, or sourcing raw materials, and your company's name is now smeared all over the internet as you recall your product (due to the co-man's inability to keep up with standards).

Or, let's say you leave the co-man, essentially putting them out of business. Then you get to be the front-page story: "Company XXX Put 47 People Out on the Street."

You might think that's a joke, but the truth is those bankruptcy attorneys are vicious. They'll find a reason to sue you.

They Don't Want You to Know How Small They Are

You probably won't realize how small they are (and how reliant they are upon you) until it's too late and you've signed a contract with them. Co-mans always try to appear larger then they really are. A quick and dirty way to assess size is by asking what their throughputs are on their lines and multiplying it by 480 minutes a shift, then 250 shifts a year, then by your toll. For example, a co-man that operates at 100 PPM at a cost of $1.00 per unit would have revenue of $12M per line.

Summary: Search Until You Find a Size Match

It's important to investigate all your options. See how your numbers look with several potential co-mans. Then make your decision.

This is an instance where taking your time and doing your research is imperative. (Unless you have an expert in the field in your pocket who already knows this information. Then it can happen in a matter of weeks. Yes, that's a shameless plug for my services.)

The bottom line: Be smart with this. Find a size match. Don't skimp or rush this part of the process.

Part IV: Preparing for the Investment

Before you decide whether you really want to be in the food industry, you need to examine your personal life and make sure you're ready for the investment. I've already talked to you about finances, but starting your own food company also requires a lot of time, energy, and personal lifestyle sacrifices that you'll want to examine before you dive into it.

You will face something I refer to as opportunity costs: The **cost** of an alternative that must be forgone in order to pursue a certain action. Put another way, the benefits you could have received by taking an alternative action.

Opportunity costs can be an intangible thing. I didn't used to think of them as real costs until I went into the consulting business. You'll only be able to do so much; there will be choices to make, and parts of your life that will go by the wayside because you chose to invest your time, energy, and resources into launching and growing your business.

You need to evaluate your life and make sure you're ready to pay the price as you pursue this opportunity. If the door of opportunity opens for you, you need to jump through it before it closes. However, you also need to know that this may cost you in other areas of your life, and you need to be willing to pay the price to make your dream happen.

My wife first came to understand the concept of opportunity costs when we were on vacation in the Outer Banks, NC, and I got my first big project. At the time, I had a full-time job, so basically I had to get the groundwork for this project done in less than nine days. I had nothing prepared and thought getting the project was a long shot.

My wife and I talked through it. We realized that this project would provide enough money to pay off a car and the rest of her student loans. That's when we decided that it was better to sacrifice the nighttime activities we'd previously had planned so I could work while the kids were asleep. I lost two full days of vacation contacting contract manufacturers.

However, that choice reaped great rewards. It all paid off in the long run.

That may or may not be the case for you. Starting a food business is risky, and it will cost you in many ways. The following chapters detail what sorts of prices you will need to pay in order to give this thing a shot. Read on to make sure you really are ready to take the plunge.

Chapter 13: Prepare Your Personal Life

In addition to having your business ideas ironed out, you need to evaluate your personal life. Those of us who are passionate, creative, and entrepreneurial can sometimes overlook the fact that those who live with us (or work with us) may not be as enthusiastic about our pursuits as we hope they will be. You also need to think through any personal issues that might get in the way before you charge ahead. This chapter addresses issues you need to consider.

The Outer Banks Vacation (That Turned Out Not to Be Such a Vacation)

I told you about my first big project, the one that required me to take time out of my vacation to the Outer Banks. That was a tough decision, but it was one that set my business into motion. It was a small sacrifice that has resulted in Right Brain Consulting.

That was also a turning point in my marriage. My wife finally realized that my "part-time hobbies" actually made money. She used to complain when I would work on my "hobbies," saying that I was just trying to get out of helping her with the kids. However, her perspective changed after I got paid for that project, which was quite successful (for me and for the client).

After that event, my wife and I communicated about the schedule each night. She would ask me, "How much time do you need for Right Brain?" and I would estimate whatever I needed to do that evening. We came to an understanding that if it was a hellish day, I would not join the family for dinner, but as a general rule I would bathe the kids and start bedtime (and then she would finish out bedtime while I returned to finish my work on my business).

If this will be your "hobby," then come to a working understanding with your spouse. Communication is key at this point in the game. You need to help your significant other understand exactly what you are undertaking. You can't say, "Hey, I'm going to spend a little time and money on this side gig I've got going on," and expect him or her to understand and be supportive. Instead you need to communicate about your plans and level of involvement before you do anything else.

Make Sure Your Partner Understands What is Involved
I'd advise you to have your partner read this book so he or she knows what exactly you are talking about when you say things like, "I'm going to produce Louie's famous hot sauce on a commercial scale." Chances are, your spouse thinks "commercial scale" is a hell of a lot less than you now think it is.

Estimate how much time and money this is going to require, and communicate that to your partner, not in vague amounts, but in concrete numbers. Remember how I said you need to sell a co-man on your idea? You also have to sell your husband or wife on it, and that may require more numbers, charts, and research than it will take to convince a co-man to work with you.

If you are tempted to lie to your partner and just hope he or she goes along with your startup venture, get ready for a divorce. Spouses don't take kindly to deceit or feeling like they've risked their entire retirement savings on some wild idea you invented.

Gauge Your Partner's Support Level
You need to find out how supportive (or unsupportive) your family really is. Most people like to appear supportive, so your husband may very well have been gritting his teeth and wearing a fake smile every time you spent the weekend

making chocolate truffles and selling them at the local candy shop, secretly hoping you would burn out on this wacky idea.

Ask your spouse for honesty. Lay the cards on the table. Then ask for support, not just for six months, but for the next few years (until you can grow your business big enough to sell it to a larger company, when you get to decide if you want to do this again or just check it off your bucket list).

Find Out if Your Partner Would Be Willing to Get Involved
You may find out that your family actually wants to get involved. Maybe your spouse is good with paperwork or research, or would love a shot at learning how to put up a WordPress site to advertise for your product. Find out if he or she will help man your booth at trade shows or if your teenaged kids want to help with some aspect of the business.

The more you can involve your spouse (and children, if they are old enough), the better chance you'll have at making this work. If your family is not interested in getting involved, you will want to come up with an arrangement that works for everyone involved. By planning ahead, you can avoid problems midstream.

This was the mistake I made and it cost me my marriage of 9 years. So please, for the love of God, have your spouse involved in some way and communicate with her or him. After we split, it completely f***ed up my business for a good 6 months.

Set Up Bumper Rails
Once you invest in starting your own business, you'll find yourself heavily invested emotionally. This means it can be easy to lose perspective and make poor decisions driven by your desperation to make this venture work at all costs.

Remember those bumper rails at the bowling alley that stop you from getting gutter balls? You need to erect similar rails to protect yourself from driving your life into the gutter as well.

Set up hard stops, such as:

- We will not touch our retirement fund.
- We will still always contribute to our IRA.
- We will quit if we get X amount in debt.
- We will give up if after X years we are still not profitable.

You may think it's foolish to set limits. You may think, "I'm smarter than that. Of course I won't do X, Y, or Z." However, you're not just setting limits to protect yourself from bad decisions.

You are setting these limits so you don't worry your spouse to death. You need your family to be assured that you won't spend the kids' 529 plans or cash in your IRA. Your partner needs to trust that you will not spend every dime you have, only to end up penniless and homeless. If you set these bumper rails in place, your family will be more likely to truly be supportive, and you need their support. So ditch your pride and come up with some limits. Then share them with everyone in your family.

Transform Yourself into Super Transparency Man (or Woman)
Anytime you feel the temptation to hide something from your spouse (an expense, a weekend spent in the commercial kitchen, a commitment to meet with a potential vendor), you need to be forthcoming with it.

Why? Because it's better to deal with your spouse's potential disapproval upfront (and then hopefully help convince him or her that your actions are justified) than to get caught later. If your spouse feels deceived, you will face more resistance than if you are always upfront.

Remember That Someone Needs to Keep the Lights On
Chances are you currently work a full-time job, and you may indeed need to continue to do so just to keep your income and benefits rolling in.

You will need to figure out how you can work around your work schedule. This might mean looking for a new job where you travel, work a flexible schedule, or can work from home (at least part of the time).

However you do it, you need to find a way to have ample privacy and flexibility. I have never worked fewer than 40 hours a week at any job I have held, but not all of those hours were put in on a 9-to-5 schedule. It seemed that about 75% of my job had to be done during work hours, but the remaining 25% could be done at night or on the weekend.

Make sure you set yourself up with that sort of situation before you get started. Or, if you are lucky enough to have a spouse who will work full time and bring in the Bennies for you, talk this through to make sure he or she is cool with you running your food business and him or her working for the Man. Whatever you do, keep your personal bottom line in sight.

Summary: Make Like a Boy Scout and Be Prepared
This is going to take time—a LOT of time. You need to be prepared for that, and you need to make sure the people in your personal life also understand and are supportive.

If you don't think you can handle spending the first two years running a business that generates no income for you, stop now. If you don't want to work 70 or 80 hours a week and on every vacation, stop now.

If you want to work for yourself and not answer to anyone, continue reading. You can make this happen—but only if you're ready to put in a lot of time and effort during those first two to three years, knowing that it will take at least a couple of years before you start seeing profits. Make sure your family is on board with you, and then prepare yourself to set sail for an adventure.

Part V: Advice for the True Do-It-Yourselfer

All right. Let's say you're a true do-it-yourselfer. Maybe you don't have $100,000 to invest yet, or maybe you are one of those people who wants to try on your own before you hire someone like me. I get it. I do. The following three chapters are my advice on how to source a co-man without me. Plain and simple, in easy-to-follow steps.

Go for it.

Chapter 14: Go In With Your Eyes Wide Open

Let's assume you've been making your product in a commercial kitchen for a while, and the people at Whole Foods can't keep your product on the shelf. You feel like a badass, and you're thinking, "There's no way I'm going to pay Will Madden a couple of thousand in fees to find me a co-man. I'm going to do this thing myself." I feel you. I get it. I hate giving money to a middleman if I don't absolutely need to do so.

I've told you already that you don't know what you don't know. Well, you also don't know how these co-manufacturers operate, and why some of them love working with newbies who are willing to fork over their money blindly.

Here are just a couple of the ways I see co-mans rip off people like you. The following advice is for those of you who are doing sub-$3M-a-year in sales. Now you'll know at least a couple of things to watch out for in a contract.

Rip Off #1: The All-Inclusive Deal

The all-inclusive sounds like a great deal. The co-man says, "Hey, don't worry your pretty little head. I'm better at buying ingredients than you, and I'll always be better at buying ingredients than you. So I'm going to charge you a dollar a bar." And you sit there and say, "Okay, it's a dollar a bar, no matter what." And maybe a dollar a bar sounds good to you, because you've been slaving away 14 hours a day, making far fewer bars than he's promising you, and your costs weren't that far off from a dollar a bar anyway.

So the deal looks good at first. What you don't know is that you'll really get screwed as your sales go up. Why? How? Read on.

Let's say you find good places to sell your product, and so you order more and more cases of bars from the co-man. However, as quantities increase, they still charge you a dollar a bar, and they buy all your ingredients a whole crap load cheaper. So while they used to spend 75 cents a bar on ingredients, now it only costs them 56 cents a bar, and they keep all that extra cash.

Also, they now have freedom to buy your ingredients from anyone they want. So if you make hard candies, they'll buy your corn syrup from an unverifiable source. Because deep in that contract, they've gotten you to sign that you're okay with them buying through a broker who doesn't have to disclose the manufacturer of the corn syrup.

That stuff can come from anywhere. It can come from Iowa; it can come from the other side of the world. It can be organic; it can be dog food. It can be anything. But it's completely masked from you because it's completely masked from them. They don't care, because they're just buying on price, and it's *your* brand, not *theirs*. So they don't give a rat's behind. They'll just buy from whatever suppliers are cheaper that week, because all they care about is their bottom line.

Not only does this cost you a lot of money you could have saved, but it also makes your traceability a real motherf***er in event of a recall. If somebody gets sick, you're up a creek without a paddle.

This can also result in an inconsistent product, which can be awful for your branding and reputation. McDonald's sells billions of dollars a year based upon consistency. You have to consistently deliver the same product to the consumer if you ever want to develop loyalty.

Lesson: Beware of all-inclusive contracts. Read the fine print.

Rip Off #2: The Set Margin/Transparent Pricing Scheme

This is another rip-off I've seen recently that absolutely amazes me. In fact, I've negotiated three exits because of this exact same type of crappy contract.

Co-mans do this to little companies, newbies, ones who don't know better. You're doing a million dollars in sales, or even just a half million, maybe a quarter. What they say is this: "We're going to give you fully transparent pricing."

And you're wowed, because you think, "Nobody else is giving me that." You're shocked, because you're thinking, "How awesome! I'll know my ingredient cost? My packaging cost? Oh, that's more than anybody else is offering me."

Then they'll say, "I will let you know exactly what price I pay for ingredients. You can even audit it. My labor? I'll charge you exactly what my labor costs me, so if my full labor costs $13 an hour and there are six people, you'll see that those six are being paid $13 an hour. You'll have all that upfront. And all I'm asking is that I make a 30% margin."

So you sit there, thinking, "Okay, so I've got 65 cents in raw materials and packaging, 5 cents in labor, and then I have 30 cents in conversion costs... Well, this is fantastic! Especially since as I grow my business, my material costs will go down."

And you're right to think that this will be the case, because as you order ingredients in bulk, and when you go from pallets to truckloads, your costs *should go down*. You're also calculating that 30% margin, thinking, "Every dime my costs go down, I pay roughly 13 cents less, so this is awesome."

But this is what happens: You're paying the co-man a set percentage of the costs: 30%. So when the co-man buys your ingredients at the most expensive rate possible, he makes the most money in making your product. This kind of contract actually encourages the co-man to buy your ingredients at the *most expensive prices*, from the *most expensive sources*, because *those high prices mean he will get more money.*

And what happens when you become bigger? Now you're ordering in truckloads. There are these things called inflation and product scarcity, because they're buying everything. They're not contracting for you; instead they're buying everything on the spot market. So if you buy almonds, today it's $3.85 and that's in season. If you buy almonds out of season, it's $5, because there are no almonds left. And they'll buy it when it's out of season, because they get 30% on top of those expensive prices.

Don't get me started on the labor. So you have those six people on the line and you are maxed out on capacity. A good co-man would look at the line and say, "Here is my bottleneck," and invest the 50k to make the widgets faster. The margin co-man won't do that because he will make less money by making product faster and with fewer people. The list of ways this deal is bad goes on.

When you're a little guy, you don't really notice this is happening to you until you come to size. And then when your ingredient costs go up a dollar, it's up by $1.33. And you start saying, "Wait a minute... you're making 33 cents more a unit, for doing the same amount of work, taking the same amount of line time, and using the same amount of people. Only now I'm paying you more for it."

But when you're a little guy with no experience, they sell you on the concept of it. They say, "Oh, when you're ordering truckloads, it's going to be so much cheaper, and you'll be paying me less. But I'll be making it up because I'll be making more units for you. Everybody wins."

The end result? You encourage them to do a bad job. You encourage them to have more people on the line than they need, to not invest in automation. You encourage them to make your product inefficiently and to buy poorly, because all that happens is they make more money.

Whenever I see one of those contracts, here is what I say to the co-man: "You know what? I'm going to fix my toll with you."

They always acted shocked. "What do you mean?"

I tell them, "I want to fix the toll."

Especially if I've got a client who's just shy of ordering ingredients by the truckload, I tell the co-man, "I'm going to fix your tolling at 27 cents," or whatever it is.

They always try to bluff me, saying, "But if costs go down, you'll lose out on this."

I just look them in the eye and say, "You believe costs will go down, but I'm willing to bet costs will go up. If you believe costs will go down, you should be ripping my arm off for this deal."

And then there's the pause.

That's when I tell them, "I do this for a living. I'm fat because I'm good at it. There are no meals missed in the Madden household. You can take this or not; I don't care. I'll find somebody else who'll give me a fixed cost. But I want full transparency *and* a fixed cost."

That's the kind of contract you want. NOT a "fixed margin and transparent cost," because that's a shit deal if I ever saw one.

With all this being said, I have recently had to enter into a fixed margin contract, but I had no choice. However, I protected the client by including several escape clauses. If the co-man pulls any stunts, I'll get my client out of there in no time. This works because I have a reputation in this business, and the co-man knows that if I pull my client, I'll also advise other clients to stay away (or pull additional clients). Without protection like that, you want to stay away from set margin contracts.

Rip Off #3: My Co-Man Loves Me

Some of my clients are in love with their co-mans, and they say their co-mans are in love with them. Then, when I find out how much they are paying, I know why their co-man's in love with them and jumps on a dime. It's because they're paying four times the market rate for something or another, something that makes it worth the co-man's time.

I had a guy who paid $1.37 apiece to have a product packaged when I easily found a co-packer who could do it all day long for a quarter. Not to mention he's no longer using preformed bags, so his cost per bag went from 14-15 cents to 6 or 8.

Remember that confections guy I mentioned? I saved as much money in packaging as I did in tolling for him. Because if you're with a good co-man, he has power over his suppliers, so you're not paying out the ass for a crappy wrapper. Instead you're paying a penny and a half for a superior packaging option.

How do you avoid getting ripped off like this? You've got to call around and compare the prices. Even if you've got a great co-man, check with others to see if you are paying the market rate.

Summary

Again, I'm not trying to be a jerk. I'm arming you with as much knowledge as I can. However, you'll quickly realize that a great deal of this requires being an insider in the industry, and that requires a lot of networking, research, and time. Put in the effort, and you'll increase your chances of getting a great co-man and decent contract. Ignore this advice, and you'll get taken.

Chapter 15: Make Sure You Are Ready

Before you approach a co-man, you will need to take the following steps. Check them off as you do them. Don't skip any steps.

1. Outline Your Process
Think through what you need to make your first batch on a commercial scale. Use the information from this book to try to plan a smooth first run. Gather information, resources and ingredients.

2. Protect Your Ass
Register with USDA or FDA or whoever is overseeing your niche. Follow the rules. Label appropriately. File paperwork. Make sure your commercial kitchen has the correct certification.

3. Hire a Chef and Get into a Commercial Kitchen
Get into the commercial kitchen, and make a batch of your product on a commercial scale. While in there, you need to use this practical experience to figure out the following:

- Your commercial scale recipe.
- Your shelf-stable, packaging, and storage issues.
- Your sources of ingredients.
- How to be FDA/USDA compliant.

Figure this all out in the commercial kitchen. Take copious notes. Ask for advice. Record everything. Investigate ingredient sources, packaging options, and both sanitation and processing requirements.

4. Figure Out the Packaging
How will you to package your product? Bag? Box? Bag in a box? The contract manufacturer will determine if it is drop-

filled, flow-wrapped, or even shrink-wrapped, but you need to have an idea of what want before you get started.

Think about aesthetics. Keep in mind, things like boxes are expensive, but they do make the product look premium, and appearances matter. Make sure your packaging matches your branding plan and fits into your budget.

5. Talk to Whole Foods
Get an appointment with Whole Foods or someone like Whole Foods (farmers market, little country store on the corner, indie grocery store, co-op). You need to sell some product somewhere so you have an idea if people will buy it and at what price point. Make the mistakes on a smaller scale.

Sell that first batch. Find out if it was easier or harder than you thought it'd be. I can tell you now that it was probably harder than you anticipated, but don't give up. Most things in life are hard if they are worthwhile.

6. Establish Your Brand
Come up with your company name, logo, images, colors, etc. Make promotional materials. Hire a designer; get your company registered. Prop up a professional-looking website. If you have industry contacts, have them provide input and direction.

7. Figure out Storage, Transportation, and Sales on a Small Scale
Get your product to the stores. How much did it cost for storage? Transportation? Shelf space? You need to have a store (for sales) lined up, a place or two that will give you shelf space. Expect to give away free samples, free product, or at the very least, highly discounted product.

Record your numbers. Try not to cry; it will get better. Learn lessons. Revise processes where necessary.

8. Repeat These First Few Steps Several Times

Wash, rinse, repeat. Make a few more batches in the commercial kitchen, and test your packaging, as well as how difficult or easy it is to follow your proposed processes. See what you want to change. See if the processing notes you made hold true.

Keep learning. Document everything. Talk to an accountant and a lawyer while you're at it, and find out what you can and cannot write off.

9. Build up Enough Capital

You need to have this before you even approach a contract manufacturer. Plan to have at least $100,000 to start. As I said before, you will most likely have to pay for everything upfront. Don't go into this "hoping" the money will show up from the heavens. Make sure you've got the cash ready. Again, all this money is not just for the co-man. It is for marketing, transportation, operating capital, consultants and such.

10. Transform Your Notes into a Presentation

Distill your notes into an intelligible, impressive presentation that will wow a potential co-man and any investors you might be able to find. Test your presentation on potential investors; see if you can get even more cash options.

Now You're Ready to Start Looking for a Co-Man

Once you've completed all these essential steps, you can finally start looking for a co-man. You're ready to make calls and knock on doors.

Do your research and start contacting co-mans. Have a pitch ready. Ask for interviews. Get referrals from people inside the industry when possible.

Summary: Use This as a Checklist

Put all 10 of these steps on your checklist and don't take any shortcuts. Sell your dream, and prove you've got everything in place to make it happen.

Chapter 16: Learn From My Experiences

I'm going to tell you about a positive experience I've had with a great co-man.

I had a sandwich business for four years and between my partner and me, we cleared in the five digits each year in less than an hour a week.

This sandwich company was very simple; it had one customer who had one distributor with six locations, and I had one contract manufacturer. Now, I'm in the contract manufacturer sourcing business, so when I did this with my own money, we did a fantastic job.

First I evaluated potential co-mans; there are guys who make to order, and there are guys who make and store.

The way I started was with a guy who made to order. We ordered a pallet at a time, and he would make 20 cases of this sandwich, 40 cases of that sandwich—all these little amounts to make up a pallet of sandwiches.

He made each pallet, and we shipped each pallet. We'd get another order, let's say this time for two pallets, and he'd make two pallets and ship them out. And that's how we proceeded for the first eight months.

My partner and I took no money for ourselves for eight months. We saved the money, and when I actually had enough in the bank to fund 900 or 1,000 cases, I started looking for a new co-man.

I wanted a co-man who could and would store onsite, because every time you touch a product, it costs you money. So what I did was find a co-man who was producing about $5M to $8M a year worth of product.

You need to understand, a co-man who does $5M to $8M is always out of money. They are hand-to-mouth all the time, and they're generally in a seasonal business like private label, schools, or food service; they're in a business that's very cyclical. So there are times in the year when they're literally dead and have no damn money. If your product is popular during the times that they're dead, you'll get a fantastic price because there's nothing else going on.

So I found a co-man who reduced my costs by about 15% (from the first co-man I worked with). But the deal that I cut with him was, "Look, I will order 1,000 cases at a time. I will pay you half upfront and half the day after you confirm how much you manufactured for me. But in exchange for this awesome deal, you have to store my product for me." And I wired him the money. I didn't even send a check; everything was wired all the time.

Now, we moved from a couple of hundred cases to 700 or 800 cases a month, depending on what time of year it was. But with him I would place $20,000-plus worth of orders all at once, and he would have his money immediately. So he loved me. It was perfect. Since he was hand-to-mouth, storage didn't matter to him because he had plenty of room. He ordered supplies the day before he needed them, because he had no money.

So when he has a guy like me who says, "I'm going to pay you for eleven pallets' worth of product, and I need you to store it and ship it as I get orders," well, to a guy like him, it's a six figures-a-year account. He doesn't mind storing the product, because he has the space anyway.

He also arranged shipping for me. We used one shipping company that delivered to six different locations for one distributor. It was golden for him, and it worked for us.

Now if I had done business with somebody who was substantially larger, like Request Foods or Little Lady Foods, they would have told me to go to hell. Because their motto is, "We make it; we ship it." Because they're doing several hundred millions of dollars a year. They're dealing with huge companies; they're not in the inventory business. You have to order full runs and then you have to take it. If I had gone with one of them, I would have had to order 2,000 or 3,000 cases of each type of sandwich.

They might have been another 5% or 6% cheaper, but those savings get eaten up quickly when I have to put it in an outside storage facility. And I have to have a truck transport it down to the end of the block at $150 a load. And then I have to pay $2.50 or $3 or $4 for each pallet coming in, then I have to pay so much a month in rent while the pallets are there, and then I have to pay $3 or $4 for the pallets going out. I have to manage the hassle of controlling the inventory and scheduling my own trucking. I have to do all of that bullshit.

When I evaluated the costs, I quickly realized it wasn't worth it. So instead of having that whole mess, my business ran like this: I had a three-week lead time with all of my customers. We would enter shipments for the next week, ship the current week's orders and invoice for the current week on Fridays. To make matters easier we invoiced directly into the customer's A/P system. In 4 years we never had a single charge back and only had 2 late deliveries.

Since we shipped from inventory I would always have an idea of what was in stock. If we were low we would enter a production order on, guess what, Friday. I would then go to the bank on Saturday and send the wire. We got to the point where I just had his account number and would deposit the funds into it.

On Tuesday he ordered his raw materials to manufacture what I needed. As a result, I always had a certain number of cases there at the ready. The whole business took me and my partner an hour a week on average. Now, my partner handled any calls from the distributor, but because we had 99% on-time delivery, there weren't calls. The best part of it all? I never met the buyer.

Why? Because I knew how to set the whole damn thing up, and I set it up right.

Summary: You Can Do It

If you simply get all the pieces of the puzzle lined up correctly, launching your food business can run smooth as silk.

But you have to get all those pieces lined up. Don't skip a step. Don't think good old Will was just exaggerating to get some business.

However, most of you won't be able to get all those pieces lined up, simply because you're outsiders. You're not inside the industry yet; you don't have the right connections.

And that's when you need to rely on your contacts and bring in experts.

Conclusion: Now My Shameless Plug

It's my opinion that you'll have a tough time finding a good co-man if you don't have extensive contacts in the industry. However, I understand that some of you honestly had no clue what this sort of endeavor entails, and now you know. I've told you the truth, and a lot of you "I Have a Dream" people are now thinking maybe you don't want to do this. And that's fine. That's good. You need to know how involved this is so you don't sink your life savings into something you aren't really ready or willing to do.

If you've realized this isn't something you can take on right now, give the commercial kitchen a try for a while. You may find that's the perfect fit for you. Sell at farmers markets; find a local store that will take a small amount of product, whatever works for your lifestyle. Have fun with it.

But if you're serious about going into this as a business, I hope you'll take my advice. Get your plan together. Make sure you prepare well. Find a way to get your hands on $100,000, and then give me a call. I'll set you up with a co-man who is right for your business, someone who will work long term. I'll save you a lot of headaches and a lot of money. Again, my fees are nowhere near $100,000, but I want to make sure you are well funded to support your business.

Some of you will still try to find a co-man on your own. You've got $100,000 (which is awesome—congrats), and you don't want to waste a couple thousand of it on a consultant.

I get it. But before you do that, I just want to tell you one more thing.

I have a lot of clients who struck out on their own. When they come to me, they almost inevitably say (as we evaluate an awful contract they are trying to escape), "Oh, I thought it was a good deal."

The sad thing is this: Those deals that looked good can cost you a lot. It might cost you a chunk of change upfront for me to do it right, but it can cost you tens of thousands for me to get you out of it (or for you to buy your way out of it.)

I have one client who had a recall thanks to his terrible co-man. Then, for seven months in a row, he had major quality complaints. The contract only stated that the co-man had 90 days to resolve the problem. It had no provision for whether the resolution was acceptable to the client. So the co-man just said, "I fixed the problem. I fixed the product." The client did not have me negotiate their exit, and it cost them in the mid-six digits to exit. That co-man almost bankrupted their business twice.

Do not hire a lawyer to negotiate the terms of your exit from a co-man as this is something they rarely ever do. Hire me. You know why? Because the people in this business know me. I bring a certain level of fear to the negotiating table, and that level of fear is rooted in the fact that I do this for everyone. They don't know what other clients they have for whom I might manage another co-man. I do a lot of work behind the scenes with companies, so they don't know who I'm working with and who I'm not working with, but they know I'm in with a lot of important clients. They're scared to screw with me.

You need the lawyer and me—we work together to manage the legalities and the business to best benefit you. I have two clients, both of whom had a bad experience with the same co-man. The first co-man had his lawyer negotiate the exit and it cost six figures to get out of their exclusive. The other guy didn't exit, but I negotiated him out of his exclusives so he is free to go whenever he wants. The second client gets a royalty for everything that's a similar product made by that co-man. So one got paid and the other paid through the nose, and the only difference was me.

I have a reputation in this industry, one that will benefit you greatly. You see, each co-man knows that I will make it my life's mission to put him out of business if he doesn't give my client a good deal. I will find every client that he has, and I will tell him what this horrendous co-man is doing, and I will move them to new co-mans for free because I'm that much of a prick.

Remember what I told you in the beginning? Yes, I am a prick, but I'm a prick who knows this business and who has a reputation for being fair and honest.

The good co-mans love me, because I'm always fair. I'll tell them where they're getting screwed in the contract, too. Which just surprises the hell out of them, because I believe in fair agreements. Fair for my client, fair for the co-man.

Why? Because then everybody benefits.

If you're a good co-man, there are so many bad ones that I *want* to bring business to you. I've negotiated contracts with you once, so I know what your hot-button issues are. I've worked with you, so I know what your shortfalls are. I know the mess that I'm getting my client into, because all co-mans suck, to a varying degree. I know all of these problems before I'm in with the problem, so I can negotiate the best deal for everyone involved.

So if I know a co-man who's good, I will bring him millions of dollars' worth of business. I have one co-man who's a bar guy, to whom I've probably brought about $25M worth of business in less than a year, $16M of it directly, $9M of it indirectly by telling clients, "This where you need to go." And I didn't even get paid for those indirect referrals.

But if I bring that co-man something that he would not normally take, he will take it, because he knows me. He trusts my judgment.

Everybody's happy, and the co-man knows that he can't screw with my clients too badly because I already have three guys in there whom I can move if he does. Plus he's thinking, "Who's the next client Will's going to bring me? Will he bring me a GMI project next?" He doesn't want me to find a new favorite place to shop.

The bad co-mans hate me, but that's cool. I never bring them clients. I just help negotiate exits from them, making sure the poor souls who got suckered into horrible contracts find the best way out of that mess.

The Bottom Line

I truly hope this book has helped you. I hope it gave you an idea of what this industry is about, and I hope it helps you make wise decisions.

I wish you the best in all your endeavors. Give me a call when you're ready to scale up, and we'll do some business together.

Made in the USA
Middletown, DE
30 May 2018